The Infamous Malaboch WAR

First publication 2017 by Footprints Press, South Africa

website: www.hiltonbarber.co.za

Cover design and page layout by Anthony Cuerden

Email: ant@flyingant.co.za

Printed by Pinetown Printers (Pty) Ltd

ISBN 9-780-620-78468-9

The Infamous Malaboch WAR

and more gripping stories from the old Transvaal and beyond

David Hilton-Barber

Introduction

The war against Malaboch has been extensively covered in articles published by the *South African Military History Society* and *South African History Online*, as well as in the *Standard Encyclopaedia of Southern Africa.* However, it was my reading of *Notes from my Diary on the Boer campaign of 1894 against the chief Malaboch of Blaauwberg, district Zoutpansberg, South African Republic* by the Rev Colin Rae (published by Juta in 1898) that sparked this fresh look at the campaign. The Rev Rae observes that "through the campaign the poor Malabochians were seldom aggressors, their attitude being nothing more or less than a gentle protest against what they considered an unjust encroachment on their ancestral rights."

In May 1894 he accompanied the commando led by General Joubert by request of the Bishop of Pretoria. "I lost no time in acceding to this request, having but little doubt as to its purport. It was, as I conjectured, to consult me as to my willingness to accompany the troops, and act as Chaplain if so required. He warned me of all dangers likely to be incurred, as well as the hardships likely to be endured. I immediately consented, as these did not deter me, promising to be ready to start at half a day's notice."

It is unclear why the Bishop wanted an Anglican priest to attend the expedition. There were only a handful of Englishmen "commandeered" and they were hardly willing recruits. Nevertheless, Rae held services at the request of Colonel Ferreira, the Acting-Commandant for the Pretoria Town Contingent. While at the scene of the campaign, "The Rev Coetsee of Pietersburg, arrived in camp and held a service for the Dutch, returning home a few days afterwards. I held regular services every Sunday morning and evening."

Rae attributed the success of his ministry amongst the troops chiefly to the faithful prayers of friends and well-wishers.

His diary was published soon afterwards; the reasons given were as follows:

In presenting the following account to the indulgence of the public, I am keeping a promise made to my comrades in the Malaboch campaign, who were kind enough to think that a published diary of events would be of interest, not only to those who were engaged in the expedition, but to a larger number who watched the proceedings of each day with anxiety, and who are deeply interested in South African affairs generally.

I believe the reasons given by Rae are no less relevant today.

Moving on to the chapter on the Ndebele nation, I am cognisant of its almost total decline and degradation in today's Zimbabwe. Once a proud state which conducted treaties in its own name with Britain and other countries, it has now been reduced to tatters. This started with the horrendous Gukurahundi, from January 1983 until December 1987, when a ZANLA crack regiment, exclusively composed of Shona soldiers trained by North Korean experts in manslaughter, killed close to 50 000 civilians in Matabeleland and Midlands. Millions more were left traumatized, displaced and disorientated after being subjected to brutal experiences including torture and rape. This was followed by the Ndebele economy being substantially converted into Shona control, financial institutions, manufacturing industry, parastatals, public institutions and the private sector all coming under Shona control. In the education sector, all schools in Bulawayo have a Shona majority in terms of staffing. SiNdebele has been relegated to an inferior language. In some churches Ndebele people are not permitted to worship in their language.

I recently came into possession of a file compiled by the late Ernest Mtunzi, resident in London and personal assistant to Joshua Nkomo until the latter's death. This collection comprises documents, reports, correspondence and analyses of the history of the Matabele people from their occupation of the territory in the mid-19th century until recent times, much of which is original and previously unpublished. This represents the start of a determined campaign to raise awareness of the plight of the Matabele people and their resolve to regain their independence as a constitutional monarchy. I am currently editing this material into a book which represents a compelling case for the plight of the Matabele people to be brought to the attention of fair-minded opinion-leaders in Southern Africa and overseas.

The exploration of the Limpopo was undertaken by a military man stirred to adventure. His aim was to find an easier outlet to the sea, and hence England, for the gold mined at Tati, than the yet undeveloped land route. Whether he was paid is moot. Nevertheless he was the first person to travel the full extent of the river to its outflow into the Indian Ocean.

The Lady Trader ended her days on a farm in the northern Drakensberg. It was called Ravenshill and I have visited it many times. It is redolent with the history of its time – Frank Eland, who was her farm manager, was killed during a skirmish with a Boer commando while serving with the Bushveld Carbineers.

The Bechuanaland piece was triggered by my visits to Francistown while researching my book on the Tati Concession. Rory Hensman's was a story to be told. I inspired my friend John Gordon Davis to write it and he visited us several times from his home in Spain. There's much more to be said about Rory and his elephants but that will have to wait for another time. I met Albert Machimani at the behest of Tito Mboweni while penning his memoir – yet to be published.

The other chapters in the book are wide-ranging and generally deal with people and events that have been under-recorded and warrant exposure.

David Hilton-Barber,

June 2017

Contents

Chief Malaboch

1.
The Infamous Malaboch War

After Chief Malaboch (Malebogo) of the Bahananwa refused to pay taxes to the new ZAR Government, the Commissioner for Native Affairs in Zoutpansberg (Northern) Division, Swart Barend Vorster set the stage for the war in December 1891 by insisting that the Bahananwa should meet the ZAR's demands.

According to one Anthony Vlotman, who accompanied Barend Vorster to Blaauwberg, the stronghold of the recalcitrant Chief on that date, the real casus belli was the insolent and hostile attitude displayed to the Commissioner when he requested Malaboch's presence for a meeting to discuss a census of the tribe. The response was: "I am *baas* upon this mountain, and shall not allow the census to be taken."

Vlotman wrote: I know the Zoutpansberg district well, having lived there on and off since the 4th February, 1888. I am well acquainted with the ways of the Kafirs, and their roguish and thieving propensities in dealing with the cattle of the Boers. Much has been said with regard to the justice or otherwise of the Malaboch War, but I think the foregoing narrative of facts points to a sufficient casus belli.

Nevertheless ten of Malaboch's head indunas then came down and, to quote Vlotman: "we were completely surrounded by considerably over two thousand Kafirs variously armed with guns and assegais. The Indunas were most insolent during the whole proceedings, and all our men stood to their guns, as we quite expected to be massacred."

The indunas repeated Malaboch's words that they did not intend paying any taxes, as they were the rightful owners of the mountain, and not the Boers.

The subsequent war against Malaboch made history for several reasons. In the first place, Malaboch, predictably, viewed the Transvaal Boers as intruders who were trying to change his way of life and refused to have his territory demarcated in 1888; nor would he have his huts recorded for tax purposes in 1891.

In the second place, this was the first time that British residents in Pretoria were "commandeered" to serve in the punitive commando. Under the Commando Law of the Republic, all inhabitants of the State, between the ages of 16 and 60, were liable for Commando service and, if commandeered, were obliged to equip themselves at their own expense with horse, saddle, rifle, ammunition, and four days' rations. As far as the "Uitlanders" were concerned, this caused somewhat of a hullabaloo. Despite these provisions in the law of the land, it was claimed, quite wrongly, that the drafting had been contrary to International law.

An appeal was made to the British High Commissioner, Sir Henry Loch, but after legal advice, he returned the "disappointing" reply that they were indeed liable for military service. Amid protests and demonstrations, a meeting was convened at the Caledonian Hall in Pretoria and the "Uitlanders Defence and Protection Association" was formed with the object of "supporting any men who might openly defy orders and refuse to proceed to the North."

The Volksraad backed off to a degree by proclaiming that foreigners might absolve themselves from military service by paying a certain levy, but the Uitlanders were determined to make an issue of the whole matter. From Johannesburg came the news that the Transvaal National Union[1] regarded the commandeering as illegal and that in the event of any Uitlander refusing to proceed to Zoutpansberg, the Union would provide funds to appeal to the courts, and would at once raise further funds to adequately provide for any distress resulting.

The defaulters, who refused to attend the Commando, were arrested and committed to trial. When the judgment of the High Court was delivered on 18 June 1894, to the effect that the men committed for trial were indeed liable for military service, these men were re-arrested for forcible removal to the front.

The Association swung into action immediately. In Pretoria close on £200 was subscribed on the very afternoon that the men left for the front. A cable was despatched to the British Government declaring the situation to be "intolerable", and calling, in no uncertain terms for diplomatic intervention. From Johannesburg the National Union cabled the British Prime Minister, Lord Rosebery, to the effect "unless prompt steps are taken to release British subjects commandeered, and prevent any recurrence, Union fears rioting and bloodshed, which it will be powerless to prevent".

Sir Henry Loch came to Pretoria by train on an official visit on 25 June (official purpose of his visit was to negotiate over Swaziland). President Kruger met him at the station and when the two entered the State Carriage, a group of men pushed forward, the carriage was unhorsed, one man jumped onto the box carrying a Union Jack and the remainder proceeded to drag the carriage to the hotel where the High Commissioner was to be accommodated, "God Save the Queen" and "Rule Britannia" being sung on the way. The President was apparently, left seated alone in the carriage

---

1. The Transvaal National Union, a political organisation, was set up in August 1892 with J Tudhope as president. The principal reason behind its formation was to further the interests of Uitlanders. The union was regarded by the ZAR as an instrument of subversion, a tool of Rhodes, Jameson and the mine owners who conspired to bring about the abortive putsch, the Jameson Raid, in 1896.

during these proceedings, and was only relieved from his "discomfiture" by the action of a group of burghers, who took the step of drawing the carriage to the Government Buildings.[2]

In a despatch to the British Government, Loch declared himself satisfied that no personal insult had been intended to the President. But the burgher population was incensed by the incident and, armed groups rode into Pretoria from the surrounding districts to express sympathy.

After diplomatic negotiation, it was established that all residents of the ZAR, regardless of protection against personal military service, were liable to be levied for contributions in money and goods; and on the same day as this became known, the commandeered men who had been forcibly removed to the front returned home. A few days later, the Transvaal National Union gave a dinner in honour of the men, and with the celebration the crisis came to an end. Thereafter Malaboch became something of an Uitlander protégé.

On the other side, of course, there was real enthusiasm for the campaign. The Rev Colin Rae[3], who was selected by the Bishop of Pretoria to accompany the Malaboch Commando to act as chaplain, wrote:

Many of the youthful members were most eager to be numbered amongst those fortunate and lucky individuals (such they considered them) whose names had already been enrolled on the list. The commando mustered on Church Square, each man equipped with a Martini-Henri rifle, a bandolier well filled with ammunition, a belt and canteen.

Some of the men had little idea of what was required, as evidenced by their general get up, a loud check suit, straw hat, and tennis shoes, with cartridge belt put on upside down, scarcely betokened a knowledge of what should constitute a smart military

2. Much of the foregoing was sourced from a thesis on the *Uitlander Movement in the South African Republic before the Jameson Raid* presented by C Webb for his BA Honours degree at the University of the Witwatersrand in1952.

3. *Notes from my Diary on the Boer campaign of 1894 against the chief Malaboch of Blaauwberg, district Zoutpansberg, South African Republic. Henry Brougham Bousfield (27 March 1832 – 10 February 1902) was a colonial Anglican priest and the inaugural Bishop of Pretoria 1878-1902.*

appearance. The crowd which had assembled was the largest, it was said, ever seen in Pretoria. The platform over the porch of the Government buildings was occupied by the Members of the Volksraad and their friends, whilst every available balcony was filled with eager onlookers, of whom the fair sex formed a goodly proportion.

Chaplain Rae's friends provided him with warm clothing, a camp-chair, a large box of "dainties", another box containing groceries, fresh and preserved vegetables, and medicines. He also asked for a horse, saddle, bridle, revolver, rifle, and ammunition, "all of which I considered absolutely necessary for my equipment But my modest requests were just as promptly though politely declined; being informed at the same time that the Government only saw its way to supply me with rations."

The Pretoria town contingent (mostly Englishmen) had no horses, and preferred keeping to the wagons rather than do stable duty. There must have been an air of excitement as the commando, headed by the band and a detachment of volunteers, marched to the Raadzaal where the Commandant General addressed them from the balcony. He congratulated the residents of Pretoria for "so nobly responding to the call of duty" and that almost every man who had been commandeered had resolved to take up arms to defend the land he lived in. (Surely the country was not under threat from Malaboch?)

With great cheering from the assembled crowd, the horsemen and wagons proceeded down Church Street bound for Wonderboom Poort where they were to spend two days.

Chaplain Rae recorded that the next day happened to be a significant one: *To-day, being the anniversary of Her Majesty Queen Victoria's birthday, we sang the National Anthem in honour of the occasion, and three loud, ringing cheers were given by Her Gracious Majesty's loyal subjects, who, although resident thousands of miles away from their native soil, were as hearty and sincere in their congratulations as any Britisher could wish to be. I may state that, during the five years I have lived in South Africa, I have invariably noticed how thoroughly devoted and attached the British subjects are to their Sovereign.*

One wonders what the other members of the Commando's reaction was to this tribute of loyalty to another country.

The chaplain was a member of No 2 Mess together with Lieutenant Sarel Eloff, Adjutant; Sergeant-Major Jonathan Malan; Sergeants Lovell Taylor and Anthony Vlotman; Corporal Gert Botha, in charge of the wagon; Corporal Frans Conradie; Troopers Austin Brook, Mauritz Preller, Durbin Brice, Charles Dargan, and Jacques du Toit; "and a most amiable set of fellows they all were."

When one of the trek oxen bolted, "Durbin Brice, the youngest member of our mess, armed with his rifle, left the wagon, and began to explore. He returned in a short time, driving before him three very good beasts which he had seized from a kraal close by."

The roads were in a terrible condition and as the *voorloope*r did not know the way, Preller, having divested himself of most of his clothes, took his place. "He trudged through the slush for hours, whooping and yelling, until we came to a place called the Pyramids." The next morning they trekked on to Waterval and from there to Haman's Kraal. The next day was Sunday and a Dutch *predikant* conducted a service. "I could not understand what was said, as he spoke in Dutch, but it was evident that an impression was made, judging by the hearty cheers that were given at the end of the speech. Although I did not leave my wagon, owing to the rain, I could hear all that passed, and was much impressed with the singing of the "Old Hundredth[4]." It was raining during the whole of the proceedings.

---

4. Old Hundred" is a hymn tune, one of the best known melodies in all Christian musical traditions. The melody receives its current name from an association with the 100th Psalm, in a translation by William Kethe entitled "All People that on Earth do Dwell."

Notwithstanding the Sabbath, some of the chaplain's companions went out shooting, others fishing, "but both hunters and anglers were rewarded with very little sport."

Onwards to Pienaar's River and then the Warm Baths; Tweefontein next and "we outspanned at a pretty little spot between Buiskop[5] and Krantz Kop. The chaplain went to look at the river they had just crossed as he had been told it was the River Nile. "I was most anxious to see this ancient river, but I have since discovered that this name had its origin from the fact that the geographers of two and half centuries ago held a fixed idea that the sources of the Nile were somewhere in Southern Africa."

At Badzynloop there was a post office where they were able to send off their mail. Their next outspan was at Naboomfontein, the Moord Drift[6]. Soon after they caught their first glimpse of the enemy's mountain "and this was our landmark for the rest of the journey."

The chaplain wrote: *During their idle time the men amused themselves by "throwing the ox hide" , a most foolish and dangerous pastime, practised by the Boers. An ox hide is procured and held by about twelve men; an unfortunate bystander is placed in the middle of the hide, and at a given signal jerked up in the air by the twelve, who catch him in his descent; some were thrown up a tremendous height and fell all of a heap, and it is a marvel to me no bones were broken. Durbin Brice, who was thrown much against his will, ricked his neck, and felt the effects for some days. This* idiotic practice *seemed to gratify the childish minds of our Boer friends, until the Commandant forbade it under penalty of a heavy fine.*

The men gathered round the wagon of Dr Tobias. *The doctor sang for the first time the "Malaboch War Song" of his own composition, all joining in the chorus*

5. Buiskop owes its name to a Coenraad De Buys who was forced to flee the Cape Colony at the beginning of the 19th Century. He fled north and with his two sons Machiel and Gabriel and a number of natives as bodyguards. Tradition relates that they incurred the wrath of a number of local tribesmen in the area and were driven to the mountain and encircled but escaped unharmed.

6.Warriors of the Ndebele chief Makapan (Makapane) massacred 23 Voortrekkers, men, women, and children, who were on a hunting expedition under Hermanus Potgieter at Moord Drift.

vigorously. He was special correspondent for the Volkstem[7]*, Pretoria, and when writing his despatches used multigraph copying-books. He invariably read these despatches to me before sending them away, and promised, on our return to Pretoria, to present me with a complete English translation; but his untimely death prevented this arrangement. Depending on these notes, I did not take such minute particulars as I should otherwise have done, and I am indebted to the Press for some details of engagements and incidents recorded herein which the doctor had better opportunity of obtaining than I had.*

War might have been in the air as far as Malaboch was concerned but there seemed to be good relations with his neighbours. The women from kraals nearby came to the wagons bearing on their heads baskets containing mealies, pumpkins, beans, sweet potatoes, *amabele*, eggs, and fowls. All these were bartered for beef and "tickeys[8]."

Mamathola[9], an old local chieftainess, with some of her followers, mostly women, squatted round the Colonel's tent. He treated her to a "substantial breakfast of about two pounds of beef, and some biscuits, which she devoured ravenously, all by herself, and then asked for more (which she didn't get)."

The next two treks brought the commandos to the base of the operation, arriving there in the afternoon of 21 June, having been on the road for 21 days since leaving Pretoria. The first engagement occurred the following morning when a patrol went some way up the mountain and burnt 22 huts. Later a stronger force - two hundred cavalry and twenty-eight infantry - reconnoitred the mountain and Austin Brook, of the infantry, related the following: —

As soon as we had set fire to some huts, the enemy opened a heavy fire on us — I should think about forty rounds — but without effect. We held our position until a

---

7. Die Volkstem (The People's Voice) was the first African-Dutch newspaper north of the Orange River. It was first published in Pretoria on 8 August 1873 under the name De Volksstem, Nieuws- en Advertentieblad.

8. The 1892 Tickey, better known in England and the Commonwealth as the threepence, is thought by many to be one of the most attractive ZAR coins.

9. The Mamathola people were moved from their original home in the north during the Makgoba campaign.

shot came from our rear. Thinking the enemy had surrounded us, we thought it prudent to retire, and on doing so, found that the shot had been fired by the guard left in charge of the horses at the foot of the hill. As we were retreating, between twenty and thirty of the enemy tried to cut us off by attacking us on our left flank, a movement which might have been successfully carried out had they exercised a little skill, as we only numbered twenty-eight, all the cavalry having left us on reaching the foot of the hill. Fortunately, their guns were of the old muzzle-loader type, and, consequently, their bark was worse than their bite.

It is not the intention in this narrative to give a detailed description of the campaign; rather to appraise the reader with eye-witness accounts and recollections of incidents. A number of skirmishes took place with losses on both sides. However, the outcome was never in doubt what with the overwhelming strength of the Boer military.

Commandant-General Piet Joubert had a considerable force under his control[10] which finally closed in around the Hoofstad, and it was only a matter of hours before it would be consigned to the flames.

Chaplain Rae: *The country after leaving Fort Jonker was very beautiful, for after crossing over a nek, the road ran through a wood, which teemed with luxuriant ferns and foliage. On emerging from this we came to a fine open plain, with here and there large clumps of bush. To the rear of us, about a thousand yards away, the mountain rose clear and barren. To our left, in which direction Malaboch's stronghold lay, the hills were covered with trees and bush so thickly that the movements of the enemy there could not be observed. The stad was situated about two hundred feet from the top of the mountain, on which was the Pretoria contingent and a number of the Marico commando. It consisted of about fifty huts nestling among huge boulders, and appeared*

10. The ZAR forces consisted of about 1 760 burghers, representing the following commandos: Zoutpansberg Commando (60), Pretoria (District) Commando (250), Pretoria (Town) Commando (150), Middelburg Commando (400), Waterberg Commando (150), Rustenburg Commando (400), Marico Commando (150). The balance was made up of detachments of the Staatsartillerie, the hospital corps and the heliograph section of the Staatsartillerie. This force was supplemented by approximately 700 men of various tribes living in the vicinity. (The South African Military History Society; Military History Journal - Vol 8 No 5)

to be inaccessible save from one direction. It was evident, however, that there must be easy communication with an enormous cave, for on our arrival, although the stad was completely deserted, yet every now and again Kafirs would come out from a cleft in the rocks, and, after firing a few shots, mysteriously disappear again.

Rev C Sonntag, who later wrote a book on the war[11], was a missionary stationed at the Berlin Mission Station on the farm Leipzig on the south-western side of the mountain. He was most unhappy about reports in the Johannesburg and Pretoria papers of his having given notice to the enemy of the commando approach by ringing the church bell. He wrote:

The reports were fabulous and altogether false. The bell, indeed, is rung every morning soon after sunrise, and has been for years; but it is only used for the purpose for which it is intended, namely, to call the people together for worship. I have done all I can to bring Malaboch to reason, even at some risk to my life. Christianity, culture, and civilisation can only be promulgated under a white Government, and no matter what may have caused the war, it matters not to me; it is not for me to judge, and so I say nothing.

This unswerving belief in the superiority of the whites, by practising Christians amongst others, is revealed in the following extract from Chaplain Rae:

Much criticism had taken place on the military manoeuvres of those who were risking their lives, not only for the safety of the country, but also for white prestige in South Africa. It mattered little what the rights or wrongs of the case were, for when once at war with the natives, every white man should know that his very existence in South Africa depends on victory for his side. Once let the natives get the idea that they can beat the whites in open war, and chaos will ensue. The blacks number about ten times as many as the whites; but, though the latter are numerically so inferior, yet it is only natural that they should take the lead. Enlightenment and civilisation must rule,

11. My friend Maleboch, Chief of the Blue Mountains (Pretoria, no date).

and it is absolutely necessary for the safety and progress of the country that the native races should be subdued and compelled to submit to the laws of the land, instead of being governed by their own petty autocratic chiefs, who are a great hindrance to the proper development of the country. Therefore, when disputes have to be settled by the fierce arbitrament of war, then especially must the result not hang in the balance.

He justified the use of dynamite in terminating the war: How anyone can discriminate between the use of dynamite and hand grenades or explosive shells passes my comprehension.

Discipline, so important in any form of warfare, was found wanting on occasion during the campaign. *One George Nefdt while in a state of intoxication, and in the presence of several Veld-Cornets and Commandants, did utter, in a loud tone of voice all kinds of insulting expressions and rebellious remarks, especially vilifying his acting serving Veld-Cornet, the said Colonel Ferreira, who was present in the said fort, such as the following: That Colonel Ferreira is drunk daily and lies amongst the boulders with a bottle of whisky; that Colonel Ferreira had sent away numbers of goats and oxen with a letter whereon there was no address; that Colonel Ferreira with the English and the Hollanders consumed the provisions which had been sent up from Pretoria for the use of everybody, amongst which were milk, whiskey, gin, corned beef, jam, and other articles, which had disappeared without a trace; and that in a loud tone of voice Nefdt had accused Colonel Ferreira of having stolen these articles and robbed the Burghers of the Commando.*

After a month of skirmishing, ambushes, attacks and retreats, the end seemed near. Chaplain Rae: *A cessation of hostilities was brought about by our people hearing a clear manly voice ring out in stentorian tones from a rock close to the stad. It was a dark night, and therefore impossible to obtain even a glimpse of the speaker, but the musical notes and distinctness of utterance carried with them their own impress of dignity, and everybody knew that it was Malaboch himself who was addressing them. What a voice it was that hushed the strife and commanded attention can be understood from the fact that it penetrated the forts behind, fully two hundred and fifty yards away, and each word was eagerly listened to as it fell from the Chiefs lips, and thus it was he spoke: "You have taken from me my women and children, my cattle and corn; my villages have you burned, and now you will not even let me have a drink of water; everything that was mine you have, wait until tomorrow and you shall have me. What do you seek in fighting tonight?"*

The following day the weak, wounded and weary hostages emerged from the caves. There were scores of dead bodies within, piled up as barriers to prevent the shells bursting inside. Then Malaboch finally surrendered. Malaboch looked about thirty years of age, standing five feet ten inches, with somewhat striking features; he wore a slight moustache and beard, and was attired in a light corduroy suit, but had on neither hat nor boots.

Rae described the Chief's attempts to end his life:

In the course of the evening Malaboch, who was sitting close to a fire, and had but just refused a pinch of snuff, suddenly plunged forward into the fire, falling on his face among the burning embers; he was with difficulty rescued from being burnt to death. Later on, about eleven o'clock, a similar occurrence took place, and he was again badly burnt; his wives now requested the guards to have him tied up, as they insisted that he was trying to commit suicide.

What to do with the prisoner? A Council of War was called together consisting of General Joubert, Commandants Erasmus, Malan, Trichardt, Pretorius, Uys, and Botha, Commissary-General Meyer, and most of the Veld-Cornets. Should he be held as a prisoner of war? Should he be shot as a deterrent to other chiefs who withheld taxes? Or would his execution serve to convince the chiefs to fight to the finish rather than face a similar fate? Eventually it was decided that Malaboch should be held as a prisoner of war until the entire campaign had been terminated.

The return to Pretoria was leisurely with time take off for shooting and fishing. At Warm Baths a dinner had been arranged for the whole contingent but owing to one of the men "attacking and half killing the coolie cook", this idea had to be abandoned.

On arrival at the capital:

A halt was called; the band formed up, and the volunteers shouldered their rifles, and the march continued through Church Street East to Church Square. It was an inspiriting spectacle. The sidewalks were crowded with onlookers from the bridge to the square; every popular demonstration that tact, thought, and affection could supply was given, including loud cheers and waving of handkerchiefs. We were utterly astounded at the enthusiasm displayed in welcoming us, and thoroughly appreciated the great kindness and self-denying efforts of our warm-hearted Pretoria friends. Banners and mottoes met our eyes at every turn; even the blue gum-trees in the Arcadia Avenue had been made use of to display the Transvaal flag. Nothing prettier in the way of decorations had ever been seen in Pretoria, and we were bid "Welcome" in English and Dutch, from many a house-front.

President Kruger was on hand to make an inspiring speech, congratulating the commandos who "willingly entered into the rocks, into the dark caves, and brought forth the enemy. Aye, even so brave were you that you would not stop at the foot of the mountain, but insisted to storm the same, in order to drive the enemy from his stronghold in the caves."

The end of it all was that Malaboch was tried by a council of war on 2 August 1894 and was found guilty on all charges. In the introduction to one of Sir Percy FitzPatrick's[12] books, the historian Deborah Lavin[13] wrote:

A fund had been raised for his (Malaboch's) defence to be conducted by the Reformer lawyer, James Leonard, and it was hoped that the trial might achieve several ends – the

12. South African Memories, originally published by Cassel, London, 1932.

13. Deborah Margaret Lavin, FRSA is a South African academic and historian, resident in the United Kingdom for most of her career.

arraignment of tyrannous native commissioners, an improved labour supply for the mines, justice for Malaboch. The trial fell through, however: Malaboch was placed under martial law, which effectively removed him from the purview of the courts, and the Jameson Raid resulted in most of his defenders joining him in detention.

He was never sentenced but kept prisoner of war until his release by the British authorities in 1900 during Anglo-Boer War 2. The chief returned to his people and ruled until his death in 1939.

* * *

Postscript

In Pretoria Gaol the Reformers and Malaboch came face to face. To quote Deborah Lavin again:

In the exchange of reminiscences, Woolls-Sampson, who had been a native commissioner in the Zoutpansberg, remembered a striking African tradition surrounding the caves in which Malaboch made his last stand. FitzPatrick recounted it all in a letter to his wife, written from the condemned cell which, from lack of other space, he shared with Woolls-Samson.

In this letter he wrote: "He sits in the sun before it gets too hot and darns the splits and rents in his 'towsies' – they are pretty far down in the list of quoted stocks now – and when it gets too warm he squats in the shade, reads his Bible and makes notes with a blunt nail on a bit of slatestone. Further in the letter, he describes the 'curious incident' related by Woolls-Sampson."

He was hunting up there one day when he came on a cave fairly large with a great wide entrance and he went in with his kafirs to rest in the cool... There were various passages leading off from this and in one corner there was a pile of stones of all shapes and sizes – from the largest that a man could carry down to pebbles. The pile looked as though it blocked up a gallery and he asked the kafirs if there was anything hidden there, and they told him the story they had heard from their parents and others, a tradition of the place! They did not know how long ago this had taken place – they had no idea of the time – but it was when the Portuguese were in the country and brought cannons and built forts and when soldiers used to walk about with iron helmets and iron or chain clothes – armour that the kafir with his assegais could not penetrate. At that time there was a fort on the hill about a mile above the cave and there a great number of Portuguese soldiers were placed; from there they traded and took slaves to the coast and generally played Old Harry with the kafirs. After a time they frightened the kafirs away from the neighbourhood so that none lived near there but a few used to come up under cover of the dense bush and spy on the soldiers and now and then make attacks on solitary men. At the time of, or rather a few days before the incident, the bulk of the Portuguese soldiers went down to the coast as an escort for the slaves and other plunder and about fifteen were left behind. Then the day came when the enterprising officer left in command determined to explore the caves so as to have a good refuge in case the small garrison should be unable to hold the fort. They closed up the fort and knowing there were no natives in the vicinity left it for the day tenantless. They went down to the cave and entered and there two umfaans who had ventured out with their sticks half from curiosity and half in play saw them enter and saw them light torches. The umfaans were too excited and frightened to stay and they scuttled back as fast as they could leg it to the kraals. In less than two hours there were hundreds of kafirs, hiding on the bush and creeping up closer and closer. Then one young man offered to creep in and see. After a few minutes he returned saying there was no one there but there was a fire in the middle of the big cave and in the big gallery there were many spoors of the Portuguese. So then they trooped in, hundreds of them, in bare-footed silence, each one carrying a stone, big or little, men , women and children; and without a whisper or a sound put the stones in the big gallery until they reached the roof. Then they ran faster and faster with their loads and regardless of noise hurled them on the growing pile and so on for hours. Once when they stopped to listen they heard voices quite clearly and the sound of stones being rolled away from the heap and they went on again knowing that they were hundreds against fifteen. And the next day when they listened they could hear no more the rolling of stones, but voices calling faintly as though miles away. But they went on again. They piled stones for a week. And at the end of the week they stopped for the stones had reached the roof of the big chamber and that was the beginning of the "big silence" which is there today. They pulled down the fort and scattered the stones over the krantz and when the Portuguese came back they found neither fort nor men nor kafirs nor any sign to guide them so they left the place as "umtagati[14]."

Lavin also refers to the discovery by FitzPatrick of the drawings of the Pretoria defences in the offices of the Pretoria Portland Cement Company dating back to 1895 (or Eerste Fabrieken, as it was then). This was evidence of the "significance of the Loch demonstrations (which) had not been lost on the government."

FitzPatrick was then a partner in H Eckstein and Company, representatives of Wernher, Beit and Company of London, later a branch of The Central Mining and Investment Corporation of London. Among FitzPatrick's responsibilities was the chairmanship of the cement company.

This aspect of his business career has often been overlooked as he is most likely remembered as the author of *Jock of the Bushveld.* This is not without merit as the book, first published in 1907, has achieved the status of a classic– more than one hundred editions have been printed and it has been translated into Afrikaans, Dutch, French, Xhosa and Zulu, amongst others. Recognition is also due to another book he wrote eight years previously – *The Transvaal from Within.* The total circulation of the English edition was some 250 000 copies and it was also published in French and

14. Extract from 'A letter from Pretoria Gaol, 1896' published in South African Memories.ß

Dutch. This brought him international fame. He met Joseph Chamberlain (Colonial Secretary), Arthur Balfour (First Lord of the Treasury, later to become Prime Minister), Lord Lansdowne (Secretary of State for War), Lord Salisbury (Prime Minister) and others and became the unofficial adviser on South African affairs to the British Cabinet.

General Pieter Joubert

Sir Henry Lock

Sir Percy FitzPatrick

Rev. Colin Rae

ZAR Staatsartillerie during the Malaboch War

King Mzilikazi, as portrayed by Captain William Cornwallis Harris, circa 1836

2.
The Founding Fathers of the Ndebele nation

Mzilikazi (which translates as "The Path of Blood" or "The Great Road") was the first King of the Matabele (the Ndebele tribe) and a descendant of the Khumalo Zulu Dynasty. After he inherited the chieftainship, King Shaka appointed Mzilikazi as the leader of one of his regiments. Mzilikazi's reputation for bravery and skill in combat grew, much to the displeasure of Shaka, who saw Mzilikazi as a potential threat and therefore hatched a plot to get rid of him. So, in about 1821, Mzilikazi and his followers crossed the Drakensburg mountains. The resultant Mfecane was a period of political disruption and population migration in Southern Africa. Was this the result of aggressive nation-building by the Zulu under Shaka and the Nbebele under Mzilikazi? Was this devastation and depopulation an excuse for white settlers to move into land which they thus considered empty? Or was it drought and environmental degradation, leading to increased competition for land and water, that encouraged the migration of farmers and cattle herders throughout the region?

Mzilikazi and his followers trekked northwards from Zululand across the Vaal River, before moving south-west from there and re-establishing himself south of modern Johannesburg. He moved north again in 1827, to an area above the Magaliesberg range, near modern Pretoria, and was there when first visited by Dr Robert Moffat, and others, in 1829. In 1832 Mzilikazi moved westwards to the Marico Valley (west of modern

Rustenburg), establishing a military capital at Mosega and royal kraals further north on the Tolane River, at Kapain (Gabeni), and elsewhere; and it was while in this area that he was visited in 1835 by Smith's Expedition, with Dr Moffat, and in 1836 by American missionaries based at Mosega and by Captain Harris. He enjoyed success in bringing other peoples under his sway, and was feared for his despotic rule. Yet Mzilikazi was soon facing another threat, from the Voortrekkers, and suffered defeats at their hands on 16 October 1836 (at Vechtkop), in January 1837 (the destruction of Mosega), and in November 1837 (the destruction of Gabeni). In 1837-38 he led his people some distance further north, across the Limpopo (and so out of modern South Africa), to the Matopo Hills and the land in the vicinity of the new capital which he founded at Bulawayo. Many, such as Robert Moffat, who were close at hand at the time, did not know that all this was happening.

The principal players were certainly Shaka in his bid to create a Zulu nation in Natal, whilst Moshoeshoe similarly created the Sotho kingdom in what is now Lesotho as a defence against Zulu incursions. At its height Zulu power extended down to the border of the Eastern Cape, which caused an exodus of refugees over the Drakensberg escarpment with a new reign of terror in Basutoland (now Lesotho) and the central interior.

Here the warrior queen Mantatisi commanded a strong force of the Batlokoa, one of the three principal branches of the Basutho race, which combined with other groups into an invading horde. An entire population was drawn into this conflict, unable to escape annihilation.

Famine swept the country, the Batlokoa were diminished and fractured, to be either wiped out or absorbed into other more powerful entities. Mantatisi returned to the Caledon Valley, where she found sanctuary in the domains of the great Sotho chief Moshoeshoe, from whose inspired leadership the Lesotho nation and people later emerged.

Over a prolonged period of time, the wandering Matabele kingdom moved in a meandering northward direction. Mzilikazi established his first royal town, Mhlahlandlela, just outside present-day Pretoria in the late 1820s. After facing a series attacks, he moved with his kingdom further northward. This took the Matabele through what was to become the "disputed territory" of Tati. At that time (the 1840s) the area had no economic or political significance. It had no towns or kraals of any size and was populated mainly by wandering hunters. The inhabitants owed allegiance to the Bamangwato chiefs, who could thus claim right by tenure. But when Mzilikazi crossed the territory with his warriors, he was no respecter of frontiers and his raiding parties roamed as they wished.

In 1862 the Matabele attacked Chief Sechele at Shoshong. Although they had the better of the fight they withdrew without consolidating their position. The Matabele claim to the Tati District was thus based on having been there in force. It was unclear who owned the District and no one cared very much.

Mzilikazi's royal town was in Matabeleland; he also called it Mhlahlandlela. Meeting little resistance from the resident Shona, Mzilikazi forged the Matabele nation from his faithful warriors, those tribes he had conquered on the way and the remnants of other groups who had fled the Zulu wars. The Amandebele, the "people of the long shields", struck terror into the hearts of many.

In Tuli – Land of Giants, De la Harpe wrote:

They soon established themselves in their new environment by subjugating the original inhabitants until they were firmly entrenched as rulers of the territory between the Limpopo and Zambezi rivers. Their Impi foraged far and wide across the land, looting cattle and capturing women and children. Between 1890 and 1902 the eastern

Tuli became the focus of numerous disputes between two powerful African chiefs, of endless spats between two unyielding political personalities and of various military confrontations between two great nations.

When Mzilikazi died in 1868 his remains were put in a cave in the Matopo Hills. Lobengula (which means "he who was sick" or "he who drives like the wind") took over. Born of a princess of the Swazi dynasty of Sobhuza I, Lobengulu overcame the opposition to his succession. His supporters prevailed and, according to Ndebele custom, he established his own royal palace which eventually became known as Bulawayo. Conquered tribes, more particularly the Shona, were forced to surrender their children, who served as slaves until they were integrated into the Matabele nation. In spite of his father's permission for the early missionaries to settle in Matabeleland, Lobengula did not allow his subjects to be converted to Christianity, fearing a power greater than his own. He merely tolerated the missionaries in his territory. Their well-being, if not their survival, depended on his unpredictable whims. The fact that he did not use the teaching skills of the missionaries to learn to read and write was a failing that cost him dearly in his later dealings with Cecil Rhodes and other concessionaires and fortune-seekers. Lobengula was reportedly a huge man, over six feet tall and weighing more than 300 pounds. He was supremely arrogant, an absolute despot who held the power of life and death over his subjects and indeed over anybody who entered his kingdom. His size and royal bearing overawed even the early white hunters, missionaries and traders who were allowed into his presence, while his own people lived in constant fear of offending him.

In his memoir (unpublished), Dr HD Crook recorded:

Although Lobengula is partial to, and courts the company of Englishmen, yet he steadfastly refuses the advances of civilisation. If he has a penchant for anything European, it is either a fine horse, a good gun or a case of champagne. The last mentioned, he has a great weakness for, drinking it from a large basin – in fact a case of Monfils is a handsome present for him.

He knows how great his power is, and what acts of cruelty he might be led into, or what folly he might commit while in a state of intoxication. It shows that he has a mind of higher order than the usual run of kafir, who are accustomed to give free rein to the passions or desires.

His ordinary attire is the national one - a kilt of one or two cat or monkey skins. If the weather is cold, he wraps a blanket of some gaudy colours around him and when taking a walk, wears a grey Inverness cape. His state costume is bizarre and burlesque in the extreme. Picture his majesty rigged out in an admiral's full-dress coat, blue cloth trousers with enormous silver stripe, a scotch cap and an old cutlass strapped to his side!

Dr Cook described Gubulwayo, the capital, as a large town built upon a high hill.

There were two trader's stores there and a Jesuit mission station inhabited by Fathers Law and Groenenburg. Father Law, an Englishman, is much respected by everybody and rightly so, for he is kind and jolly to all, and has not a scrap of humbug about him. Twenty five years ago he was a lieutenant in Her Britannic Majesty's navy and but for Jesuitism might have been an admiral by this time. I fear the Jesuits will do very little, and as yet have not made a single convert. It is doubtful that they will remain long in the country. Upon their arrival they only asked to be allowed to stay at Gubulawayo until the rainy season was over, and then proceed to the Zambezi, but they have long exceeded that period, and Lobengula, who is not much prepossessive in their favour, may at any time request them to leave the country.

Lobengula spent a great deal of his time on his farm where he and his entourage lived in traditional huts, built with long thin branches driven into the ground, bent with raw bark into a dome, then thatched with long grass, with the floor smeared with cow-dung.

The King's hut was especially well-built and the floor had so continually been rubbed with iron stone that it resembled black marble and possessed a fine polish. Mr Fairbairn, who had been trading in Matabele country for some years, undertook to introduce us to his majesty and also conduct our business for us. With him as our "cicerone" we passed through the cattle kraal and entered the enclosure of the King's hut, inside of which, lolling on a blanket, and surrounded by several of his favourite wives, was Lobengula, son of the great Mzilikazi, King of the Matabeles. Being desirous to enter the hut, we did so (on our hands and knees for the doorway was no more than two feet high) when the King saluted each of us with a cordial shake of the hand. We seated ourselves on the floor and he then enquired our names, asked our positions in life and whether we were married. Answering these questions fully, he then cross-examined us upon the Zulu war, on which subject he seemed very well informed, and thought it was close to a miracle that Cetewayo, the great lion, could have been subdued and captured.

Fred Barber [great-uncle of the author], who led a hunting party to Matabeleland in 1875, followed the accepted procedure of calling on the King wherever he happened to be at the time, reporting themselves, exchanging civilities and presents, eating fat meat, drinking beer and making friends. Barber recorded his impressions of the royal court:

We were told that "Loben" was down in his lands supervising his many spouses and slaves, who were preparing the soil for the next season's mealie crops. Proceeding thither, we espied the burly potentate sitting on the top of a small rocky eminence, while below and about him, perched upon their hams, were about forty majakas (young soldiers), his bodyguard. It was evident that the King was in good humour, as they were chattering and laughing and noisily discoursing. Below them in the fields, a considerable number of women and slaves were cultivating the soil with hoes.

Lobengula joked about his name:

"You say your name is Barber? Why, that's my name." ("Baba", signifying "Father" was the name by which he was addressed by his people.)

He asked us all about our journey, and whether our oxen were healthy and not affected with any contagious diseases. What was the object of our journey? Were we hunters or traders? And he chaffingly asked us if we were not frightened to go into the hunting country, as lions and elephants were dangerous things to shoot.

After a while, he invited his visitors to the kraal to drink beer and have something to eat:

As he strode along, followed by his shouting and singing majakas, we could not but admire his jaunty and dignified carriage, powerful build, and massive limbs. Around his waist was a great apron of cat and monkey tails, completely encircling his loins. Bar sunshine, a few ivory rings and brass armlets were his only attire. His hair was worked up to an apex, surrounded on the top by an oily shining ring, or sekethla. His face was pleasant in conversation, with a humorous twinkle in his eye. He was ready-witted and loved a joke, a grand savage, and every inch a king, a fit ruler for the savage hordes over whom he had to wield a firm and stern sway.

Arriving at the kraal, he climbed upon his wagon and perched himself on the front wagon box, while we found sitting places where we could, on the wagon pole and stumps of trees forming the kraal. Gradually the kraal filled with indunas, headmen, and followers. Maidens handed round Buchala beer in closely woven baskets. A big vessel was handed to us, to which we did ample justice. The King's beer was always good! Then followed a huge flat-bottomed wooden dish with a savory joint of beef. The King cut this into chunks as big as a leg of mutton, using his left hand as a fork. A chunk was handed us. We pulled out our pocket knives and hacked it up and "chawed". It was splendidly cooked, we were hungry, and hearty old hunters found no difficulty in dining in this primitive manner, and in no time our hunger was appeased.

Next morning after breakfast an extraordinary apparition approached our wagons. It was some time before we could analyse it. We thought it was some new arrival, some gigantic Dutchman bound for the bush veld. It stalked into our bush fence round our wagons. Lobengulo! Lo and behold! What a metamorphosis! The cat and monkey tails had given place to a complete suit of brown moleskin, his huge limbs and feet were encased in Wellington boots, and a spreading brown wide-awake felt hat covered his sable brow. It was absurd, ridiculous. Loben in European clothes was no longer a king, the dignity of his savage majesty had gone. He was no longer picturesque, but he was quite satisfied with himself. I have no doubt but that he thought he was paying us a delicate compliment. Had it not been for the great respect, if not awe, with which we regarded him, we should have burst into laughter, but he was not a man to be laughed at, ridiculous though he make himself. We reserved our mirth for another time.

We sat him down on our strongest chair and contemplated him nervously, lest he should go through it, and were greatly relieved when it held. We produced a bottle of French brandy, and had to sip some from his glass to show that it was not poisoned. Then we drank to our better acquaintance. Then we chatted and brought out and showed him our elephant guns and had some rifle practice with them. My brother and I gave him a silver-mounted revolver and a silver mug with a glass bottom. He was delighted both, especially the mug, which he hugged and carried away In his hand and used all the time we were there, and was still using on our return from the hunting country. Then he wanted to see the coloured stuffs, and we pulled out a number of highly coloured plaid shawls and rugs, some of which he took a fancy to. We presented him with these.

Soon after their arrival, the great dance of the first fruits was celebrated. A small white tent was pitched at the gate of the *sekotla*, in front of which, in his armchair, Lobengula sat, a white umbrella held over his head, surrounded by councillors, indunas, white men, and attendants, reviewing and inspecting his army.

This was a magnificent sight, a great dusky phalanx of sable warriors, seven or eight thousand strong, each regiment under its own induna and distinguished by different coloured shields covered with bullock hide. Marking time with measured tread, they chanted solemn dirges and sang war songs, striking their shields with assegais, while distinguished warriors would bound from the ranks, spring into the air, stabbing and thrusting as if in desperate combat, each thrust signifying a man he had killed. Sometimes in his excitement a man would make too many stabs, and be greeted with howls and shouts of derision from his companions for lying, when he would retire crestfallen to the ranks.

The King would also go through a ceremony of throwing an assegai, applauded by terrific shouts from thousands of men. Great numbers of cattle were killed to feed the warriors. (Sometimes a wild bullock would escape after being wounded by a badly directed thrust from an assegai, and he would career over the veld, pursued by a dozen shouting warriors, who would bring him back exhausted to be slain for dinner.) The first day and night, the flesh was spread out and hung on the kraals and fences to propitiate evil spirits. Next day the hungry warriors would be given permission through the witch doctors to feed, the spirits being appeased. Then a scene of roasting and gorging half-cooked meat would commence, that was more like an orgy of ghouls than human beings, tearing and fighting for the meat and rubbing their heads and ebony bodies until they shone with fat.

Within a radius of fifteen or twenty miles were the King's cattle stations, where he often spent weeks of his time. As soon as he was tired of one place, he inspanned his wagons, one of which was filled with ivory, and moved from cattle post to cattle post, accompanied by his court and bodyguard. The cattle are divided among the posts or stations according to colour. (At one station are the red, at another the black, and so on.) Each herd is in charge of the induna (headman) of the town. All the cattle in the country are the King's, and no beast is killed without his permission. Every case of sickness or death is immediately reported to him, and special messengers come running in in hot haste to report. They also report deaths of people, but the death or loss of a beast is of far more importance than that of a human being, the latter being merely a matter of small significance.

Every affair of the nation is reported to him by messengers. He is the chief magistrate and gives judgment without hesitation in all matters of life or death. What the King says is final, and there is nothing more to be said. Small matters are left to the indunas of the kraals.

"Great political cases are discussed by meetings of the indunas and headmen, who sit in debate for days sometimes. Each one has his say, the King listens, and when the subject has been thoroughly thrashed out, gives his judgment. Cattle are killed, beer handed round, and everybody praises the wisdom of the King, who sits on his wagon box in front of his travelling wagon, cracks jokes, spins yarns, and entertains his people. When the meat is all gorged and the beer drunk, and the King retires to sleep, the people disperse to their homes, with loud shouts and praises for the King."

Barber continues:

At Bulawayo the traders had built a number of houses and stores, and there are usually about fifteen or twenty whites living there always. The elephant and other hunters collect here in the beginning and in the end of the season. Permission to hunt must be procured from the King before you can enter the hunting veld. The hunting season commences as soon as the worst of the fever season is over, end of April, and the general ruck of hunters get back about November, at which time the weather becomes hot and the rainy season sets in. The hunters disperse to their different homes in the Transvaal, Kimberley, etc. Many stay in Bulawayo, where they sell their produce of ivory, feathers, skins, etc. The majority of the hunters are Boers, and traders, English.

Crook described Lobengula's seat of power as follows:

Gubulwayo, the capital, is a large town about nine miles from his farm. We often rode there, passing through miles of corn gardens, and obtaining a fine view of the station, which is built upon a high hill. There were two traders' stores there and a Jesuit mission station inhabited by Fathers Law and Groenenburg. Father Law, an Englishman, is much respected by everybody and rightly so, for he is kind and jolly to all, and has not a scrap of humbug about him. Twenty-five years ago he was a lieutenant in Her Britannic Majesty's navy and but for Jesuitism might have been an admiral by this time. I fear the Jesuits will do very little, and as yet have not made a single convert. It is doubtful that they will remain long in the country. Upon their arrival they only asked to be allowed to stay at Gubulwayo until the rainy season was over, and then proceed to the Zambezi, but they have long exceeded that period, and Lobengula, who is not much prepossessive in their favour, may at any time request them to leave the country.

According to De le Harpe, Lobengula used the eastern Tuli as his royal hunting ground and believed he had a valid claim to it. But the area was also claimed by Khama the Great of the Bangwato by virtue of his people's actual residence there.

In contrast to the Matabele King, Chief Khama, an ancestor of Sir Seretse Khama (the first president of an independent Botswana), though equally powerful in his own right, was far less warlike and far more amenable to the minor tribes living within his kingdom. The chiefs of these various tribes were permitted to govern their own people and retain their own customs, while their young men were absorbed into the Bangwato regiments, becoming assimilated into the ruling clan in this way. Khama was taught by Lutheran missionaries and baptised into the Christian faith in 1860, his education standing him in good stead, especially when Bechuanaland was overrun with concessionaires after the discovery of gold on the Witwatersrand to the south. Many less literate tribal chiefs were tricked by unscrupulous Europeans in their quest for concessions to prospect for metals and minerals, and who later claimed that they had been given the land by the chiefs and not merely the rights to use it.

Lobengula and Khama were old foes, and the dispute over the ownership of the eastern Tuli dragged on for years. Transvaal's President Kruger took every opportunity to stir up strife between the two chiefs, thinking it would aid Boer ambitions north of the Limpopo River. And Khama was most concerned that the British would decide in Lobengula's favour, which would "bring the lion to the very door of my hut". "He was convinced that Lobengula would allow traders to sell liquor in the area, which would jeopardise the complete ban he had placed on its sale in his territory. In a letter to the Commissioner of British Bechuanaland he anxiously communicated his concern:

"I fear Lobengula less than I fear brandy. I dread the white man's drink more than all the assegais of the Matabele, which kill men's bodies and it is quickly over."

Finally, in 1895, the British formally awarded the area to Chief Khama. The settlers' defeat of the Matabele in 1893, in which the Bangwato played a part, no doubt helped resolve the matter.

Following the occupation of Matabeleland by Rhodes's Pioneer Column, a party of Lobengula's warriors raided a Mashona village near Fort Victoria, threatening a camp of British settlers In July 1893. The Matebele War followed the British High Commissioner's authorisation to then present military force to respond and indeed to continue the advance until all of Matabeleland was occupied and under strict British control. Lobengula and a small remnant of his once powerful impis were driven north of the Zambezi River.

In his book *Rhodes – a Life*, Sir James McDonald describes the now very ill Lobengula's last hours:

He felt his end was near, and calling together those faithful indunas and warriors who still remained with him, he said: ". . . go now all of you to Rhodes and seek his protection. He will be your chief and friend." To the fighting men present he said: "You have done your best, my soldiers; you can help me no more. I thank you all. Go now to your kraals and Mjan [the General of all of Lobengula's Impi], the greatest of you all, will go to Rhodes, who will make things all right for you." To all of you I say: "Hambani kuhle. Go in peace!" Before twenty-four hours had elapsed, Lobengula was no more and Mjan in due course reached Bulawayo and gave this account of his last hours.

Although Lobengula was not the cause of the war which led to his downfall, he could well have countered it better. The first weakness shown by Lobengula was that, instead of arming his force with the assegai only, he sought strength in the rifle. Cetehwayo once said: "The man who invented the gun was a coward," and Isandalawana demonstrated how formidable a Zulu army was when armed with assegais, even against a force with guns and cannons. Mzilikazi established this powerful kingdom with the assegai; Lobengula destroyed it by the clumsy use of rifles.

Just fancy what folly: a steamboat with cannon on the Zambesi, and 1 000 rifles with 100 000 rounds of ammunition for his 20,000 warriors! Of course he intended to use the steamboat against the Barotsi and the rifles against Khama, but when he went out to war against the company he wanted to fight them with the arms he had received from them: that was the chief cause of his defeat. Had Lobengula stuck to the assegai, and had he attacked the incoming force in the mountain passes and forests, especially by night, the result would have been different, at least in the beginning.

This was his second mistake; instead of stopping the enemy on his inaccessible borders with his chief regiments, he presumptuously enticed them into the open country, and attacked them there at first with light young regiments, probably thinking that, having been enticed into the country, he could easily annihilate them with his veteran regiments.

It is also to be borne in mind that Matabeleland is a territory with no roads and almost inaccessible borders. Really there was only one waggon road made by the hunters, crossing the country in a slanting direction from

Mangwe on the south-west across Bulawayo to the Hartley Hills on the north-west. The Transvaal lies to the south, to the south-east and east is the impenetrable Matopo range, to the north the unhealthy lowlands of the Zambesi. In fact the country could only be attacked from two sides, on the east from Mashonaland and on the south-west from British Bechuanaland through the impregnable Mangwe pass.

If he had concentrated his forces on these two points, 900 or 1000 volunteers would not so soon and so easily have conquered the country. The Mangwe pass for twenty miles runs through a mountain range full of granite koppies and bush. Then Lobengula put only one regiment at the entrance; and had Colonel Goold-Adams marched in there, probably not a single man would have returned; this all the men who served with him as volunteers acknowledge. Luckily the Colonel had Selous and Raaf with him, and these marched by a detour to the north-west in order to draw out the Matabele, who were actually presumptuous enough to go six miles out in the open to attack the Colonel. There they had to be beaten back, and still had Selous and Raaf not been present the result might have been fatal to the volunteers. For the Matabele were beaten off" (and this was at the time not publicly mentioned) only after four waggons with provisions and ammunition had been taken and burned, and Selous, by whom chiefly worse results were prevented, had been wounded. And still that regiment held the pass and would have held it, had not the reports of the defeats sustained by the Matabeles against the Mashonaland column discouraged them, and caused them to retreat voluntarily and leave that pass open to the invaders.

* * *

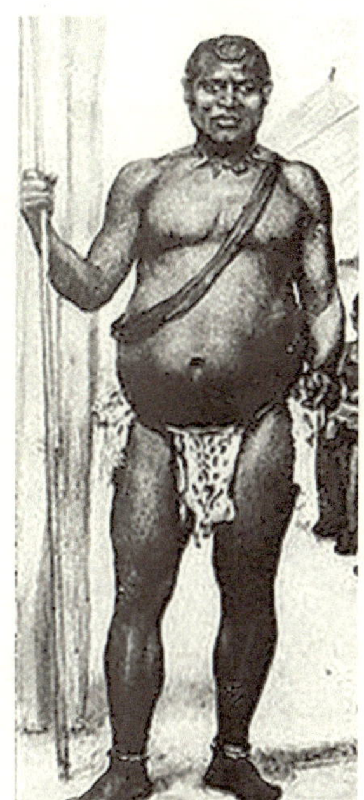

Lobengula Khumalo

The King in his 'bath chair'

Lobengula holds an indaba outside his sleeping hut

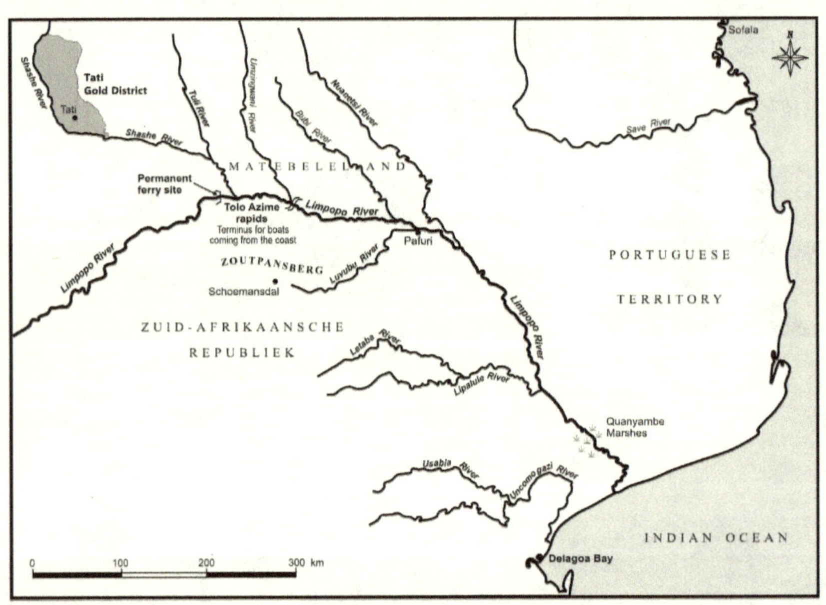

Sofala
N
Tati
Gold District
Tati
Shashe River
Shashe River
Tuli River
Umzingwani River
Bubi River
Nuanetsi River
Save River
MATEBELELAND
Permanent
ferry site
Tolo Azime
rapids
Terminus for boats
coming from the coast
Limpopo River
Pafuri
Limpopo River
ZOUTPANSBERG
Luvubu River
Schoemansdal
PORTUGUESE
TERRITORY
Limpopo River
ZUID-AFRIKAANSCHE
REPUBLIEK
Letaba River
Lipalule River
Quanyambe
Marshes
Usabia River
Uncomogazi River
INDIAN OCEAN
Delagoa Bay
0
100
200
300 km

3.
Exploration of the Limpopo[15]

The first proper exploration of the Limpopo River was undertaken by Captain Frederic Elton in 1870. This remarkable man was the son of an officer in the Bengal Army. At the age of 17, when the Indian Mutiny broke out in 1857, he himself joined the Bengal Army. He saw active service with the relieving forces at Delhi and Lucknow which won him the Indian medal with two clasps. In 1860 Elton volunteered for service in China, and was present at the taking of Peking and other engagements, receiving the China medal after the campaign. Soon after gaining his captaincy (98th regiment), he left the British service, and in 1866 joined the staff of the French Army in Mexico during the reign of the Emperor Maximilian.

On his return to England at the conclusion of the war, he published an account of his adventures, entitled *With the French in Mexico*[16].

In 1868 Elton went to Natal, and occupied himself in travelling about the colony until 1870, when he undertook a long journey of exploration from the Tati gold district down to the mouth of the Limpopo. His narrative of this journey, accompanied by an excellent map, was published in volume XLII of the *Journal of the Royal Geographical Society.*

The idea of making a voyage down the Limpopo first struck me on seeing the river in January 1870. I discussed my plans with Mr Baines FRGS[17] *who was sanguine as to the result of such an exploration, his theory being that the waters of the Usabia*

---

15. Extract from The Baronet and the Matabele King, The Intriguing Story of the Tati Concession, David Hilton-Barber, 30 Degrees South, 2015.
16. *With the French in Mexico*, Originally published in 1867.
17. Thomas Baines, the English artist and explorer of British colonial southern Africa. In 1858 Baines accompanied David Livingstone along the Zambezi, and was one of the first white men to view Victoria Falls.

[probably the Sabie] and the Limpopo joined and emptied themselves into the sea by a river which could prove to be navigable. Although the theory eventually proved an incorrect one, I must say in justice to Mr Baines that his encouragement and the kindness with which he furnished me with all the information at his disposal, in a great measure decided me to undertake the journey.

Elton approached Levert, the managing director of the London and Limpopo Mining Company at Tati in March 1870, proposing that an expedition along the Limpopo: " . . . would lead to the discovery of a shorter route of practicable communication – partly by land, partly by water – between the Tati River and the sea coast, and consequently effect an important saving in time, and a considerable reduction in the heavy expenses of the carriage of goods by wagons from Natal via Potchefstroom – the circuitous route in general use."

Levert agreed and ". . . a flat-bottomed boat, 13 feet long with masts, sails, oars etc was successfully constructed at the Tati; donkeys were ordered from the Transvaal; an interpreter was engaged; saddle bags were made; and a man from Umseila's tribe, acquainted with the coast country and the lower Limpopo was enlisted as major-domo." As permission had first to be sought from Lobengula, Elton and Levert visited the king's kraal the following month. Approval was given for a road to be constructed from the Shashi to the Limpopo and Lobengula also promised support on the projected journey from the tribes over which he held power or influence. However, the departure was delayed by a serious setback:

"Through the thoughtlessness of one of the miners, a quantity of blasting powder was exploded, the sparks falling from his pipe into the chest used as a magazine, in which he was searching for a letter. The log-house was instantly enveloped in flames, and it was with difficulty, scorched as we all were by the explosion, that any of us escaped.

"Mr Levert was very severely burnt; the author of the misfortune was killed; two miners, the interpreter and myself were more or less injured and the remaining days of May and the month of June found us all under the hands of the doctor. July commenced, no wagons arrived from the Transvaal, no donkeys were to be found, and the interpreter engaged for the journey, impatient at the long delay, broke his agreement, and left the Tati. Everything appeared to go against the expedition."

But Elton was made of sterner stuff and, disregarding the threat of tsetse fly, determined to start off with pack-oxen instead of donkeys. He set off on 6 July with his boat and baggage in a wagon. He kept careful notes of the countryside, vegetation and animals: *Lions are numerous and prowl about the river banks by night, in search of the game that they know must be forced by thirst into their clutches. Guinea-fowls, grey and red partridges, francolin and bush pheasants troop down in the cool of the evening across the sands; the rhinoceros, buffalo, gnu, koodoo, pallah, zebra, giraffe, Harris buck and tsessebe, hidden in the shade of the bush during the day, before daybreak and at sundown turn their heads towards the water, The elephant travels rapidly from one river to another, the constant war waged against him by the hunters keeping him nervously on the alert, and the ostrich - already rare in the land – chooses an open grass glade where a good view of all approaches can be obtained. The hyena, packs of wild dogs and the tiger with flocks of vultures and the eagle are the scavengers of the land - an immense nursery-ground for big game.*

Elton encountered serious problems in getting carriers for the boat – he had to send the wagon back to Tati because of the difficult terrain – and he continued with pack oxen and boat bearers, eventually reaching the Limpopo. He soon realised that navigation on the smaller rivers was out of the question.

"The Tuli, though a permanent river is, owing to rapids, falls and its rocky bed, impracticable for any description of boat; neither is the Shashi of any practical utility regarded as a means of water communication, except perhaps during the rainy season, when the absence of rocks would permit a large-sized boat to descend this latter river to the Limpopo with safety. The scenery on the Tuli is wild and striking; large baobabs, tamarind and fig trees border the stream and numerous rapids and a remarkably rocky causeway near the kraals of Masiringi, over which the river falls in a succession of cascades, and races in a boiling torrent down a deep gorge into a lovely valley."

He identified the site for a pont and a permanent ferry over the Limpopo close to the Tuli River mouth in the event of a road being opened from Tati. Further down, the Limpopo formed "a broad deep stream about two hundred yards in breadth, fringed with large trees and thick underwood". The boat was readied for launching and the oxen were sent ahead on the left bank of the river: *At dawn on 1 August [1870] I began my voyage, Selika's men shrieking with delight and excitement at the sight of the first boat that had ever been launched on the upper waters of the "great river", for up to the very last moment they would not believe that I seriously meant to carry out my plan*s.

Elton must have felt some relief too and for the first day the progress down river was unimpeded: *Crocodiles were seen in numbers; a large troop of buffaloes broke from their covert in the reeds and halted to survey us from the lower slope of the hills on the left bank. From the opposite range on the Zoutpansberg side, a species of wild fig, taking root everywhere among the interstices of the rocks, hung in long, graceful tendrils, and appeared to cover the favourite hiding-places of numerous monkeys, who loudly chattered their surprise at our unusual appearance. One or two large fish eagles rose from the shadow of the cliffs with shrill screams; an occasional cormorant, a few pairs of Egyptian geese and graceful blue and white herons lazily watched our approach; and towards evening large flocks of hornbills passed in their clumsy flight over our heads. Twenty yards' walk opened up a spectacle well calculated to make us shudder at the peril we had so narrowly escaped. A magnificent fall dashed down into a yawning chasm right ahead of the channel where we had stopped the boat, and formed one of a succession of cataracts by which the river precipitated its waters through a vast rent in the land to a lower level. Torrents of pale green water tore through the narrow passage beneath our feet, foaming and breaking in clouds of spray, over huge boulders.*

Elton's plight was severe. There was no additional assistance at hand and their attempts to dislodge the boat only resulted in it being swept down the chasm, crashing on a ledge of rocks and being knocked to pieces: "I consequently abandoned the Freeman – a most unfortunate loss." ["The Free-man" was the name of the boat].

From the central plateau, the river descends to a lower level through this deep lateral gorge, known then as "Tolo Azime". Indeed, this gorge was the terminus for boats coming upriver from the coast, as experienced by Captain G A Chaddock some 14 years later. In 1884 Chaddock steamed for 340 miles up to the Pafuri (Levubu) confluence, where it enters Portuguese territory.

AH Keane[18] writes: "The Chaddock expedition was perhaps somewhat in the nature of a tour de force, for it has not been followed by others, and for all practical purposes the Limpopo would appear to be accessible to steamers of moderate draft for little more than fifty or sixty miles from the coast. In any case, all navigation is arrested at the Tolo Azime rapids, some distance above the point reached by Captain Chaddock."

Elton, nevertheless, soldiered onwards, on foot with three pack oxen and his four followers. They crossed and re-crossed the river, generally

18. AH Keane, *The Boer States: Land and People*, Methuen, London, 1900

being avoided by the natives. However they did occasionally encounter "a rude but hospitable population, rich in pumpkins, millet, maize, dacha, ground nuts and sun-dried locusts - the Makalaka element predominating."

He kept detailed notes of the various tribesmen he met. At the lower end of the scale were the "knobnuizen": " . . . a wretched specimen of humanity, and a living testimony in favour of the Darwinian theory – without a vestige of clothing, tattooed with a line of knobs, bearing a striking resemblance to warts, extending from the roots of his wool perpendicularly down the forehead to the end of his nose. These unfortunate people inhabit small huts hidden away in the bush, and live by their bows and arrows, or upon edible roots. Intensely black in colour, with the everted lips and prognathous jaw exaggerated in character, they bear on their persons all the outward signs of want, abasement and degradation. They are of inferior stature, small-limbed with large hands and feet, pot-bellied and spindle-shanked."

In contrast were the Matabele: "The warriors were ten in number, well-armed with assegais and large cowhide shields, and attired in a picturesque war-dress of feather bonnets, leopard skin moochas, with tippets, armlets and anklets of gnu's tails, and accompanied by about 15 carriers. They presented a rather formidable appearance."

Their route took them inland to the Levubu River - "a clear, brawling river with deep runs like a Devonshire trout stream" - where they came upon a large village under Chief Makuleke, before regaining the Limpopo. This was fertile country to some distance beyond the Nuanetsi. Here the kraals were neat, clean, well-built, shaded by trees: The hemp plant is largely cultivated, and the men are passionately addicted to 'dacha', with both sexes indulging inordinately in snuff and beer, and the consumption of these three luxuries occupies the greatest part of their idle time."

Elton felt that the Limpopo, from the Nuanetsi to the Lipalule, ". . . will afford, even at the driest seasons of the year, a navigable channel; and it would be quite practicable to use the river as a way of water communication, cargoes being towed in flats by steamers with a light draught of water. The right bank also presents great facilities for the construction of a road, and the district being rich and alluvial – wild cotton grows luxuriantly, large timber borders the river, and the crops adjoining the kraal yield abundantly – it would, if colonised by Europeans, rapidly become a fertile and important centre, monopolising a considerable trade with the interior."

They encountered the "dreaded tsetse fly" but without any bad effects on the oxen. Elton considered the dangers of the disease highly exaggerated (but he was there in August, which was a winter month). He was, however, bothered by "mosquitoes, midges and other diptera and parasita – the curse of African travel – which were nightly unwelcome visitors, increasing in annoying power as we approached the coast, and as the hot weather began to set in."

The expedition left the Limpopo at the junction of the "meeting of the waters" of the Lipalule, a point already named by St Vincent Erskine, who from to penetrate any distance inland from the Sofala coast since the Portuguese gold-seekers of the sixteenth century, and had he had also explored the region between the Limpopo and the Pungwe several years earlier. At this point Elton directed his course in a straight line towards Delagoa Bay: "I had by now more than connected my journey with his [Erskine's]; and as single-handed and without a boat I could make no practical survey of the lower waters and the bar, I determined to strike across the Lipalule, cross the Uncomogazi [Komati], and gain Delagoa Bay; reserving the mouth of the Limpopo until I could visit it from the sea, and prove whether the bar would permit light draught of water vessels to enter the river."

Elton detoured round the Quanyambe marshes where there were, " . . . considerable incrustations of salt which the inhabitants of the adjacent villages collect and roughly purify and send up the Uncomogazi, and barter for tobacco, dakha, millet and fowls." After 52 marching days and an estimated 1 500 km he arrived in pouring rain at the gates of Delagoa Bay, "where the sentry appeared to have some scruples in admitting a party headed by a white man dressed in an old leathern kilt and gaiters, considerably travel-stained and rather excusably over-excited at his safe arrival at the sea-board".

The principal trade at this port "consists in the purchase of ground nuts and gingelly seed, orchilla weed, beeswax and a little ivory against which are bartered powder, guns, striped blue and white cottonades of Swiss manufacture, beads and brass wire.

"Things have changed mightily since in 1823 the Leven and Barracouta saw a caravan of 1 000 traders with 300 or 400 tusks and many cattle arrive at the factory".

Elton described the town as "built on a whaleback sand flat, nearly surrounded by water at low tide, and entirely commanded by the neighbouring heights from which the natives from time to time have threatened the Portuguese with apparent impunity. It is surrounded by a wall, and defended by three bastions fronting the land, each bastion mounting a gun on a traverse platform".

Elton reckoned that the length of the stretch of the Limpopo River from the "meeting of the waters" to the sea was 120 miles. The upward trip was navigable: "Numerous canoes and vessels have frequently crossed the bar and proceeded up the river for a considerable distance; however great care will be necessary on first entering the river. The mouth of the river being navigable, and the reach from the Nuanetsi to the Lipalula being certainly practicable for light draught of water steamers, I have no doubt whatever that below the Lipalula an abundance of water will be found. "I will undertake, with six months' preparation, to run steamers and flats to the Nuanetsi (or Levubu) in fifteen days, and connect with a wagon road (or with camels) via Zoutpansberg to the Tati, a journey which should be made easily in fifteen more. That is thirty days in all. A road already exists from Schoemansdal to the kraals of Makuleka, and has frequently been travelled by wagons. The unhealthiness of the Limpopo and coast has, I am sure, been greatly exaggerated. None of my party suffered from fever, and we were in very hard work all the time, had no tents, and never entered a kraal at night, but slept in the open air on the river bank, and that too without any waterproof sheets and with a single blanket apiece (all our bedding was lost in the boat)."

This fascinating adventure and the subsequent proposal must have been given serious consideration by the London and Limpopo Company. However, the goldfields never lived up to their earlier promise and regrettably what could have been a new trade route from Tati to the coast never materialised. George McCall Theal in his *History of South Africa* records that: "From a commercial point of view his journey was a failure but it resulted in a great improvement in the map of South Africa."

Elton, meanwhile, continued his career with some distinction. He was a consultant for the Governor-General of Mozambique and the Sultan of Zanzibar for a telegraph cable from Aden. Soon afterwards he was appointed by Sir Bartle Frere (who had been sent by the British Foreign Office to negotiate a treaty with the Sultan) as Assistant Political Agent and Vice-Consul at Zanzibar, and two years later he was promoted to the office of British Consul in Portuguese territory, with residence at Mozambique. He made several journeys into the interior of Mozambique and Nyasaland to explore the lake and surrounding country, visit various chiefs connected with the slave-trade, and ascertain the possibility of a route from the north end of the lake to Quiloa, an island near Zanzibar. His mission to the chiefs and the circumnavigation of the lake were successfully accomplished, but on his return journey he contracted malaria and died on 19 December 1877 at the age of 37. He was buried about two miles from his last camp, under a large baobab tree, where his companions marked the spot by a large wooden cross, and carved his initials on the tree which overshadows his grave.

* * *

Elephants crossing the Levubu River (Photo Fanus Grove)

4.
The Lady Trader

In 1894 a remarkable woman settled on the mountain top overlooking the territory of Queen Modjadji. Sarah Heckford, born into an aristocratic family in Ireland in 1839 (her grandfather was the Governor of the Bank of Ireland), defied convention. Tragedy had marred her early life. She was sickly and malformed with a slight hunchback. Her mother died when she was six, and her father committed suicide four years later. Her education was completed under the guidance of her uncle who emphasised "accomplishments and social graces". She learnt to play the piano and to paint in watercolours. Her destiny, however, lay beyond the confines of upper-class expectations. She wanted to lead a useful life and she heeded the clarion call of the Women's Movement which, in 1858, published the first edition of *The Englishwoman's Journal.*

She took to visiting the poorer areas of London, comforting the women and giving sweets to their children. Her sorties into the slums upset her uncle but he was unable to change her ways. As she wrote in her diary at the time: "I was absolutely my own mistress and bound to obedience of no one but myself." When the great cholera epidemic swept London in 1866, Sarah volunteered as a nurse and was assigned to the Wapping Street District Cholera Hospital near the docks. There, she met the 23-year-old Nathaniel Heckford, a brilliant doctor, whom she was to marry. Charles Dickens, writing on the couple, stated: "No romancer that I know of has had the boldness to prefigure the life of this young husband and young wife in the Children's Hospital in the East End of London."

Yet the pioneering work Sarah did in the field of child welfare was only the first chapter in a life of astonishing adventure. Dogged once more by misfortune, Sarah was widowed after barely a decade of marriage. When her husband died, she decided to seek her fortune in South Africa. By then, she had given away most of her money. She arrived at the time of the first war of independence and endured the siege of Pretoria. Here she became a governess and then a farmer; later she became a transport-rider, trading goods with hunters and miners in the Lowveld.

Her biographer[19] later recorded: "A widow of forty, small and slight, lame into the bargain, subject to severe attacks of malaria and probably tubercular as well, hardly seemed ideally suited to a rugged, often dangerous life of travel by ox-cart across the still turbulent countryside of the Transvaal."

Sarah Heckford was indomitable!' She transported the goods she bought in Pretoria as far as the territory of the Lobedu and the Klein Letaba goldfields, trading equally with the diggers (who paid in gold), the

19.Vivien Allen.

trek Boers and the natives. She was on good terms with all with whom she came into contact. She had been trading for some years before deciding to move permanently to the northern Transvaal. For a short while she even became a miner. She camped at the goldfields and pegged her own claim near the Birthday Mine where she panned gold worth £40. However, she gave up this task and rented a portion of the farm Platland near Mooketsi.

It was always Sarah's wish that her cousin, Sarah Eland, born Featherstonehaugh, should join her in the Transvaal. Mrs Eland had been deserted by her husband when her son, Frank, was a toddler. In 1890 Sarah and Frank, then 17, were able to sail out from England to join her cousin. Sarah bought the farm Sterkwater for £47 from Bisse Philip Sanderson Reed, the first English-speaking settler in the area. It was an "occupation" farm the ownership of which required residence on the property. This was a regulation of the ZAR to attract settlers to these areas. Sarah registered the property in the name of Frank Eland as Ravenshill. The farm, in extent 1 000 acres, was on the western edge of the Woodbush Mountains. Some 20 acres had been cleared for cultivation but the rest was mostly covered by indigenous mist-belt forest. One side bordered on the land of Modjadji, which encouraged her from the trading point of view. They initially lived at Platland while Sarah Heckford camped in her wagon at Sarah Heckford

Ravenshill, supervising the building of a house there. Soon Frank came to help her and the house was completed by the end of the year. She became friendly with Fritz Reuter, the German missionary at Medingen, situated within Modjadji's territory. Sarah Heckford, as to be expected of such a character, had met the "Rain Queen", Modjadji II, who was then an old woman (she died in 1896) and became her friend and adviser. The Boers were furious and called Sarah "Modjadji's lawyer". There was general unrest in the area and General Piet Joubert was about to engage with chief Makgoba after which Modjadji would be "seen to". Sarah was appalled as Joubert had previously written to Modjadji saying "she and her people will in no way be molested as she had been obedient". At the time of the Makgoba campaign in 1894, all non-combatants were ordered into laager at New Agatha or Houtbosdorp. However, Sarah Heckford and Frank's mother Sarah Eland chose to remain at Ravenshill where they felt safe. Sarah recorded later that she had received a message form Queen Modjadji to the effect that they were both women. "I need have no fear as she counted me as her sister and her people as my children, and they would defend me as such." A large commando appeared at Ravenshill where they bivouacked while others surrounded the location even though Modjadji had obeyed all orders and remained peaceful. The order came to disarm her people and Frank Eland went alone into the location to advise Modjadji to deliver their arms to Sarah at Ravenshill. The commando confiscated several thousand cattle as a fine on Modjadji and in taxes. The old queen was further humiliated by being taken in person to Joubert's camp. Sarah wrote in a letter: "I met the poor old woman on her way back to her location and shook hands with her and expressed my sympathy. She is very old and was all of a tremble." Modjadji's punishment was for her "harbouring refugees from Mahupa" (whose tribesmen had been raiding white farms) and for allowing many of her people to live outside her location. Meanwhile, Sarah Heckford's health was in decline. She was happy that she had provided a home and a means of livelihood for Sara Eland and Frank. She now wanted to turn her attention to another project that had long since occupied her mind – that of farm schools. On one of her visits to London, Sarah Heckford met Dora Scrimgeour, a young lady of 26 who developed a "crush" on Sarah. Her father, John Alexander Scrimgeour, was a wealthy stockbroker. On Sarah's return to the Transvaal, the two exchanged correspondence in the form of diaries which they sent to each other. Years later, Dora sailed to South Africa to join Sarah. She had invested money at Sarah's behest in a farm near Naboomspruit, Tobiaszynloop, and wished to inspect the property. It was a sound deal as years later it was bought by the railways and the siding Tobias is still there. The two women journeyed on to Ravenshill. Dora was soon to fall in love with Frank Eland and within a short while they were married. (Their daughter, Dora Maud, was born in England where her mother had repaired during the Anglo-Boer War. While she was away, she was widowed – see below.) Sarah left her enlarged "family" at Ravenshill and returned to Pretoria to launch the Transvaal Women's Educational Union enrolling members – equally English and Boer women – to lobby their menfolk and the government to provide for the education of young children on the farms. Sarah saw that the future of the country depended on the children growing up together. Then the Anglo-Boer war broke out and Sarah was staying with her friends at their farm in the Magaliesberg. They moved to Pretoria when the British occupied the capital and Sarah offered her services to the British authorities to reorganise and reopen the schools that had been closed down at the outbreak of war. She also worked tirelessly on her project for farm schools. She produced a lengthy report for the Education Department and also started another project for adult education – what if the children were to have schooling and their parents had none? However, she fell seriously ill and it was thought she was dying. She took ship for England and when she arrived found herself a minor celebrity. Letters she had written had been published in *The Spectator* and had attracted a great deal of attention. She was overwhelmed with requests to speak on her experiences. Simultaneously, Emily Hobhouse's first broadside against the concentration camps was published. Sarah fired back against what she regarded as preconceptions by people visiting South Africa for a few weeks. An article was published in *The Times* which quoted Sarah as rejecting Miss Hobhouse's assertion that she was well qualified to give an opinion on the state of the concentration camps. "In a country distracted with war no camp can be otherwise than unhygienic." The emotional battle between these two eccentric Englishwomen, each absolutely sure she was right, provided fine entertainment for newspaper readers and attracted impressive support for both sides. In the midst of this contest, Sarah was stunned with the news of Frank Eland's death in action not far from Ravenshill. He had joined the Bushveldt Carbineers and was shot by the Boers while trying to recover the body of Captain Hunt, of whom more later. Sarah addressed a number of meetings on matters of education in South Africa, on opportunities for women and on the war. She wrote articles for many publications including *The Times*, the *Pall Mall Gazette* and *The Spectator* appealing for funds for education. However, her health continued to deteriorate. She became blind in one eye and partially lost the sight of the other. She contracted pneumonia and on April 17 1902 she died, two months before her 63rd birthday. An obituary in the Pretoria News reads: "She was a worker among women whom we can ill afford, as a community, to lose. She took an advanced and more serious view of women's conditions in the economy of the state than is customary and her death is a serious loss indeed to the capital." Another obituary, in *The Times* of London dated April 21 1903 stated: "It is not an extravagance to call Mrs Heckford one of the most extraordinary women to whom the British nation has given birth." In her own words, she "leaped the barriers of young-ladydom, though they were high and armed with sharp spikes". The well-researched biography of Sarah Heckford by Vivien Allen, *The Lady Trader*, has been the source of much of my information. The Allen family emigrated to Pretoria in 1966. Vivien, who had studied at the Royal Academy of Music in London, became a freelance critic of music, theatre and books for the *Pretoria News*. She contributed a series of articles, "Old Pretoria", on the buildings still standing that had been there in the days of Paul Kruger and also about the people who had lived in them. This led to her researches on a number of interesting pioneers and early visitors to the city and this series, "They Came to Pretoria", was to give birth to the biography published by *Collins* in London in 1979.

* * *

East London Children's Hospital

Queen Modjadji
(sketch by Charles Astley Maberley

Emily Hobhouse

Modjadji Cycad Reserve

Rev Fritz Reuter

The Baobab tree is one of the curiosities described by Oates in his journals: "The tree was perfectly gigantic in girth, thickening as it got higher, though of no great height. It was swollen and bloated in a most extraordinary manner ... Though still flourishing, it was a mere shell, and, looking in at a hole in the side, I saw that it was open to the sky at the top. Inside is a good-sized chamber, strewed with minute bones of rats or some small mammalia. No doubt generations of owls have long had their abode here; one flew out at our approach."

5.
Francis Oates, forgotten naturalist

The death of Francis Oates in Botswana is all but forgotten. But the late Ilona Somerset recorded this sad event in her book, *The Seven Lost Trails and Outdoor Adventures in Eastern Botswana.*

Oates was not a daredevil game slaughterer, avaricious gold miner or freebooting farmer, but a naturalist. His observations have proved invaluable to the natural world and it is fitting that he lies buried in the Far Interior.

In a report to Sir Theophilus Shepstone, Captain EE Patterson described the capital of the Bamangwato country in 1878, as "badly watered by a small source becoming a sand river in the Kloof. There are far preferable sites for a town, but this was chosen for reasons of strategy, the hills on three of its sides being steep, rugged, and easy of defence."

Frank came from a well-to-do family in Leeds and he matriculated at Christ Church, Oxford, but a respiratory disease forced him to leave after three and a half years. He spent four years living quietly and regaining his strength and in 1871 he sailed for Guatemala and California. Oates's journey to the Americas whetted his appetite for collection and he planned a visit to the Victoria Falls and Matabeleland in 1873. With his brother William and a party of traders, Oates began his adventure in Pietermaritzburg and travelled through Shoshong to Matabeleland. Swollen rivers stopped his attempt to reach the Falls and he relocated to Shoshong to refit. At Shoshong he hired van Rooyen, one of the Interior's most successful guns, to guide him to the Falls and hunt elephants on halves (sharing the kill). Redwater Fever broke out among his oxen and Oates returned to Tati to refit. A frustrated Oates had to return to Tati for a second time due to Redwater Fever.

Frank Oates had crushing luck. He attempted on three occasions to reach Victoria Falls, and in his impatience to see the Falls he took the suicidal step of travelling in the wet season. He left his wagons at Pandamatenga and walked to the Victoria Falls with Dr Benjamin Bradshaw, a former ship's doctor on an American liner. Oates and Bradshaw returned on foot from the Falls to Pandamatenga[20] on 13 January 1875. Two of their Kalanga servants were sick with fever and Oates was feeling seedy with a persistent headache, the first alarm bells in the onset of malaria. Dr Bradshaw, John MacKenna and George Westbeech escorted the rapidly ailing Oates to Tati, but about five miles from the Shashe, Oates died quietly. The ground in the area is very stony and they did not have any tools with them, but Piet Jacobs was hunting nearby and they sought help from him. The hunter found an old game pit and without fuss or ceremony, the remains of Francis Oates, FRGS were buried.

Before reaching Tati, Bradshaw noticed that Rail, one of Oates' dogs, was missing and he sent a few Bakalanga back to find the animal. Rail was found guarding the grave. The devoted dog had walked eighty miles through country fraught with predators to return to his beloved master. John Mackenzie took custody of the deceased's possessions and he notified the Oates family of Frank's death. Rail was sent back to England where he died on the fifth anniversary of his master's death, and three weeks later Rail's brother Rock was dead.

20. "The Old Hunter Road", opened up by George Westbeech in the 1870s, went some 400 miles north-west through Pandamatenga (today the site of a border post between Botswana and Zimbabwe) to the Zambezi.

The Oates family hired a Geordie named Gilchrist to fetch Frank's possessions and lay a headstone on the lonely grave. Piet Jacobs took Gilchrist to the spot, which had been marked by a cairn of stones. A small white stone bearing the simple inscription, "Frank Oates, FRGS of Meanwoodside, Leeds, died 5th February 1875 aged 34 years" was placed at the grave (which then disappeared from sight in the remote bush)

In 1934 a member of the Oates family contacted the Pioneer Society in Bulawayo and sought their help in locating the grave. The grave was found by James Haskins[21] of Francistown who had a store near the drift. No sign of the headstone was found and Haskins[20] identified the grave by its unusual mound of stones. He reported the location to the Pioneer Society and suggested that the Society erect an iron cross, similar to those used by the Bechuanaland Protectorate Police.

As World War II drew to a close, Frank Oates, another member of the Oates family, contacted the Society as he wished to visit the grave of his great-uncle at the cessation of hostilities. Sir Robert Tredgold, a grandson of John Smith Moffat and Chief Justice of the Federation, placed it on the priority list for after the war. R Tapson, the Native Commissioner at Plumtree, spent many years searching for the grave, and in 1955 a Kalanga named Liburu guided the Commissioner to the site. Tapson was overjoyed and summoned Sir Robert from his Judicial Bench in Harare. They travelled to the site in a Land Rover with Liburu and on their arrival they met a very old Kalanga. The old gentleman told them that he had erected the cross and later the railing on the instructions of a white man from the police in Francistown. However, the old man pointed to a mound of rocks some 50 yards away and told the Commissioner and Judge that the bones of the

21. Haskins, one of the pioneer traders at Tati, arrived from England in July 1897. He established a general trading business, the Francistown Supply Company which supplied mine requirements. This grew into J Haskins and Sons, a name as native to the country as Chobe bush-buck and tsamma melon in the Botswana of today.

man lay under the mound and not under the railing.

John Walsingham of Francistown solved the mystery. During a very heavy storm some years later, flood waters carved a groove beside the mound of stones, exposing the remains. Walsingham and his brothers-in-law James and Billy Haskins reinterred the remains of Francis Oates at the iron cross erected by the Pioneer Society. Sir Robert Tredgold, in the company of Alan Henderson and my father-in-law Owen Somerset, visited the site in the 1960s and I have Sir Robert's original hand-drawn sketch map of the Westbeech Road from Kazungula to the grave. It is remarkably accurate.

The curator of Supa Ngwao Museum in Francistown, Catrien van Waarden[22], tramped the area in the 1980s to find the grave and she warned me that locating it was no easy task. I flew over the area in 1995 and took GPS readings over the grave that proved spot-on.

Frank's brother, William, who came to Africa with him, hunted and collected specimens in Africa, India and in the Americas until his death from typhoid on Madeira. The Oates family were true adventurers. On 17 March 1912, after the bitter disappointment of finding Roald Amundsen's Norwegian flag fluttering in the Polar breeze to indicate that he had lost the race for the South Pole, Captain Robert Falcon Scott, R.N., made the most famous entry in his diary. A "brave and gallant gentleman" with badly frost bitten feet knew he would hinder his companions, so he walked out into a blizzard and died in the frozen waste of the Antarctic. The brave Guards Officer's name was Captain Lawrence Oates and, not surprisingly, he was a nephew of Frank and son of William.

* * *

22. Historical and cultural anthropologist, Van Waarden is the author of many books on Botswana, including *Prehistoric Copper Mining in Botswana* and *The Oral History of the Bakalanga of Botswana.*

Lawrence Oates

Frank Oates

(Engravings based upon watercolours by Frank Oates, published in Matabele Land,1881.)

Frank Oates's book

James Haskins

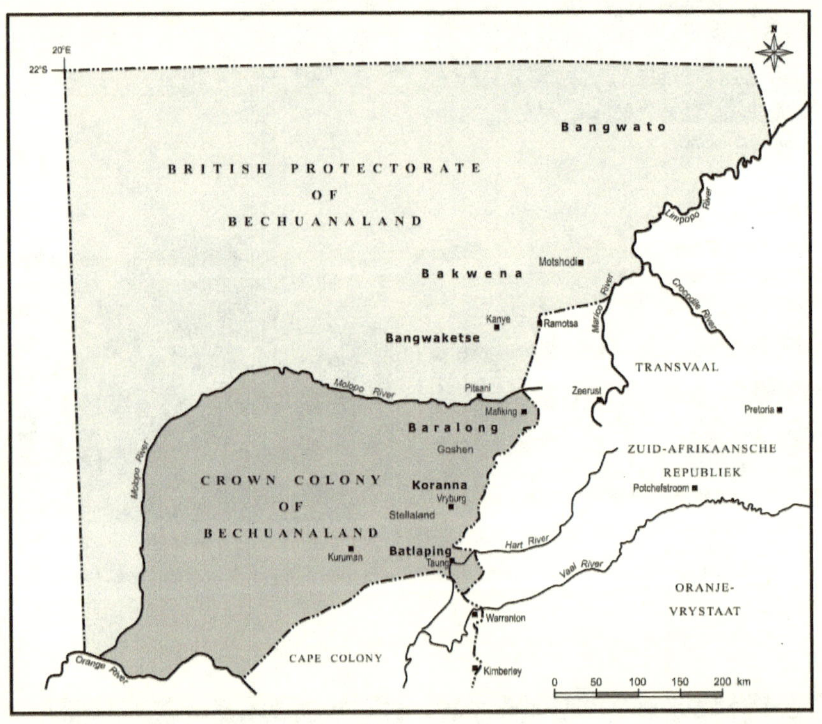
20°E
22°S
Bangwato
BRITISH PROTECTORATE
OF
BECHUANALAND
Limpopo River
Motshodi
Bakwena
Crocodile River
Marico River
Kanye
Ramotsa
Bangwaketse
TRANSVAAL
Molopo River
Pitsani
Zeerust
Mafiking
Pretoria
Baralong
Goshen
ZUID-AFRIKAANSCHE
REPUBLIEK
Molopo River
CROWN COLONY
OF
BECHUANALAND
Koranna
Vryburg
Potchefstroom
Stellaland
Hart River
Kuruman
Batlaping
Taung
Vaal River
ORANJE-
VRYSTAAT
Warrenton
CAPE COLONY
Orange River
Kimberley
0 50 100 150 200 km

6.
Annexation of Bechuanaland

Why did Great Britain add Bechuanaland to the Imperial fold in 1884/5?

Was it the threat of a Transvaal-German alliance affecting Britain's political control and trading interests of the sub-continent? The successful Transvaal rebellion in that year had led to a determined effort by the Boer leadership to expand its eastern and western borders and to seek to regain the total independence of the 1850s. Buoyed by their success, the Transvalers, although they already held a great and rich but thinly populated country, began to push outwards, and especially to threaten the native tribes in the barren region of Bechuanaland. Boer extremists also began to look about for allies, and believed they had reason to expect aid from Germany.

This followed the German entry into the "Scramble for Africa" with Chancellor Otto von Bismarck sending FA Luderitz to set up the colony of Angra Pequena, in present-day Namibia, the small bay where the Portuguese explorer, Bartholomew Dias, landed in 1487.

This, incidentally also angered the Cape politicians who regarded this area as part of their domain. Islands off the coast of Angra Pequena, rich in guano deposits, were annexed by Great Britain in 1867 and added to Cape Colony in 1874. The colonial secretary , Lord Derby , supported by the High Commissioner for Southern Africa, Hercules Robinson (later the first Baron Rosemead), felt that the Cape Government should be responsible for protecting the Tswana chiefs and, more importantly , the "Road to the North".

An interesting detail was that one of Sir Hercules' officials, Evelyn Ashley, suggested that Britain should accede to the request of the Cape Government for Britain to take over Basutoland as a colony while part of Bechuanaland should be incorporated into the Cape Colony. In 1867 and 1868, most of Moshoeshoe's land was overrun by Boers from the Orange Free State. Moshoeshoe appealed to the British for protection, and on 12 March 1868 his country became a British protectorate, and the borders of Basutoland, now Lesotho, were established, although some of its previous territory was lost, including fertile farming area west of the Caledon River, which was ceded to the Boers. After his country became a British protectorate, Moshoeshoe wrote:

"The whole of my tribe, all the Chiefs of Basutoland, and myself more than anyone, are all glad. It matters little to us to which Colony Basutoland is to be annexed, so long as we are under British protection and rule."

Basutoland, as the Kingdom was called at that stage, was transferred to the Cape Colony in 1871. This state of affairs led to increased tension, and in 1880 the "Gun War" broke out. The result of the conflict was that in 1884 Basutoland became a colony of its own under direct rule from London, where it remained until its independence in 1966.

Did British public opinion support Cecil Rhodes's dream of a great united state of South Africa? This was to be a British South Africa with equality of treatment between the races, as in all the British lands. Rhodes dreamed of a great brotherhood of British communities, governed by British ideals, girdling the world, perhaps dominating it and leading it to peace and liberty.

Christopher Paulin[23] examines the political situation in the region from 1877 to 1895. He maintains that it was the threat of disruption of the labour supply to the diamond mines that finally persuaded Britain, despite the prevailing unwillingness to increase imperial responsibilities, to annex Bechuanaland. Whatever the real reasons, history records that Britain established a protectorate over Bechuanaland at the request of native chiefs: the motive of this annexation was not suspicion of Germany, for this suspicion did not yet exist, but the desire to protect the native population.

The influence of the missionaries should also be taken into account. AJ Dachs[24] was convinced that the secular force of British imperialism was seen by the missionaries as a factor in their success: "Already from the middle of the nineteenth century they called upon the British government to preserve their mission field and their hosts from Boer expansion. More than that, David Livingstone deliberately directed his efforts to the north to occupy the interior before the Transvaal settlers could enter their claims to 'the exclusion of those of missionaries'. And, as one, the missionaries developed the slogan and doctrine of the 'Road to the North' as the basis of their appeal to the British Government."

As the Rev John Mackenzie observed in 1876: "On the whole, the old feudal power of the native chiefs is opposed to Christianity; and the people who are living under English law are in a far more advantageous position as to the reception of the Gospel than when they were living in their own heathen towns surrounded by all its thralls and sanctions."

23. *White Men's Dreams, Black Men's Blood: African Labor and British Expansionism in Southern Africa, 1877-1895* Trenton: Africa World Press, 2001.

24. AJ Dachs book, *Missionary Imperialism, the case of Bechuanaland*, Journal of African History, Vol 13, 1972.

Mackenzie, resident at Shoshong since 1862, had advised Chief Matsheng to appeal for British rule over his Bangwato. In 1868 he wrote in Austral Africa: "Great interest and excitement were created in the years 1866-1868 by the undoubted discovery of gold in Mashonaland, Matabeleland, and different parts of North Bechuanaland."

In connection with the gold mine discovered at Tati, the chief at Shoshong, Matcheng, addressed a letter to Sir Philip Wodehouse, who was then Governor of the Cape Colony. The purport of the chiefs letter was that if large numbers of Europeans were to come northwards to dig this *tsipi* (metal), the chief would expect the Representative of the Queen, as head of the white men in South Africa, to send an officer into the country to control them, and prevent them from taking the law into their own hands.

Governor Wodehouse, in his response, requested: "The best information you can obtain as to the real extent and position of these gold fields, and the proportion of gold found in the ore; also as to the number of Europeans that may have come to you, and from what quarter; also as to the time occupied in travelling from the borders of the Cape Colony to your place of residence and to the gold fields - the best season for the journey, and the nature of the country through which the road passes - with any other information that you may think likely to be of use."

How the good Governor expected the chief to provide the answer these questions is beyond belief: it would appear he was fudging the issue! Nevertheless, by the early 1880s a number of politicians in Britain began agitating for the annexation of Bechuanaland, on the grounds that British rule was needed to restore order among the warring Koranna, Batlapin and Baralong tribes.

Robinson, who in 1884 had signed the London Convention for the British government with Paul Kruger, the new state president of the South

African Republic, adopted a hard-line approach the following year. The convention limited the expansion of the Republic to the west and when the republics of Stellaland and Goshen were proclaimed he regarded this as a serious contravention. Of course the Keate award was the cause of this. Robinson, aware of the necessity of preserving this country – the main road to the north – for the British Empire, determined on vigorous action. John Mackenzie and later Cecil Rhodes were sent to secure the peaceful submission of the Boers, but without immediate result, partly owing to the attitude of the Cape Ministry. Robinson's declaration that the advice of his ministers to patch up a settlement with the filibustering Boers was equivalent to a condonation of crime led to the expedition of Sir Charles Warren and the annexation of Bechuanaland early in 1885.

J Ramsay[25] writes: "The Protectorate was imposed on the Batswana. No chief asked for it an only three - Khama III of the Bangwato, Gaseitsiwe I of the Bangwaketse and Sechele I of the Bakwena - were consulted afterwards. Khama welcomed it, whereas Gaseitsiwe and Sechele reluctantly accepted. In so doing, all knew from the experiences of other Africans that it was futile to resist Britain's military power."

On 13 May 1885 Khama signed a document, drafted by Mackenzie, in which he stated: "I, Khama, Chief of the Bamangwato, with my younger brothers and heads of my town, express my gratitude at the coming of the messengers of the Queen of England, and for the announcement to me of the Protectorate which has been established by desire of the Queen, and which has come to help the law of the Bamangwato also. I give thanks for the words of the Queen, which I have heard, and I accept the friendship and protection of the Government of England within the Bamangwato country.

"Further I give to the Queen to make laws and to change them in the

25. The Establishment and Consolidation of the Bechuanaland Protectorate, 1877- 1910.

country of the Bamangwato, with reference to both black and white. Nevertheless I am not baffled in the Government of my town or in deciding cases among my own people according to custom; but again I do not refuse help in these offices. Although this is so, I have to say that there are certain laws of my country which the Queen of England finds in operation, and which are advantageous for my people, and I wish these laws should be established, and not taken away by the Government of England. I refer to the law concerning intoxicating drinks, that they should not enter the country of the Bamangwato whether among black or white people. I refer further to our law which declares that the lands of the Bamangwato are not saleable. I say this law also is good. Let it be upheld and continue to be law."

* * *

Scene in Bechuanaland (Fred Barber)

Bismarck in 1881

David Livingstone

Rev. John Mackenzie

Chief Khama III

Sir Hercules Robinson

Interior of Kimbery Mine

7.
Stellaland and Goshen

The developments that occurred in and around Griqualand West had a major impact on the history of the sub-continent. When John Wodehouse, the first Earl of Kimberley, took over in the Colonial Office in 1870 as Secretary of State for the Colonies, he became embroiled in the controversy surrounding the ownership of the recently discovered diamond fields in the area which later became known as Griqualand West. The diamond -mining town of Kimberley, where some of the most precious gems were discovered, was named after him.

Kimberley was largely responsible for the appointment of Robert Keate (who was Lieutenant-Governor of Natal at the time) to arbitrate in the dispute over the ownership of diamondiferous land. The controversial outcome, the so-called Keate award, later led to the British annexation of Griqualand West as a Crown Colony on 27 October 1871 and the appointment of Southey to administer the area. An unintended consequence of this award was that a section of territory north of the Vaal River was cut off from the South African Republic.

In October 1878 120 farmers who lived in this disputed area sent a petition to the High Commissioner of the Cape, Sir Bartle Frere, asking that they be re-annexed. But this was not complied with. (In the previous year, Frere had recommended that the Imperial authorities annex to the British dominions the whole territory south of Portuguese Angola from the Atlantic coast to the Transvaal border. This would certainly have involved considerable expenditure but would have significantly changed the history of Southern Africa.) As a consequence of the Keate award, these farmers and all the other whites living in the territory east of the Kalahari were now living under the jurisdiction of competing Griqua and Tswana groups.

Lieutenant-Colonel Charles Warren was instructed by the High Commissioner in 1878 to lay down boundary lines between the contending clans and induce them to live in peace with each other. Notwithstanding his confiscation of about a thousand guns from different unruly clans, he was not successful in restoring order. Warren then arrested the highest-ranking Batlapin chief, Botlasiti, who was imprisoned in Kimberley. Further disputes resulted in a skirmish with the Koranas and old quarrels flared up, and it was clear to observers that order could only be restored by a strong ruling power. Britain appeared to be compelled by these circumstances to assert her sovereignty over Bechuanaland, but the time was not ripe.

In October 1881 war broke out between the Batlapin chief Mankoroane, whose principal kraal was Taung, and Massou, the Korana captain who lived at Mamusa (Schweizer-Reineke). Each chief invited whites to assist him, promising as payment a share of the booty and a farm when the war was over. There were hundreds of men in South Africa eager to take advantage of such an opportunity to acquire land and cattle. The British authorities regarded them as filibusters and freebooters but there was no intention on the part of the mercenaries to kill those on the opposite side – in fact very few lost their lives in operations. Their principal aim was to secure a peaceful outcome. Most of those enlisted by Massou came from the Transvaal but there were 60 deserters from the British regiments among them. Mankoroane's allies were mostly from the diamond fields and the towns in the Cape Colony. Hostilities continued for nine months until, in July 1882, peace was concluded between the two contending chiefs and their people, largely through the mediation of the Transvaal authorities. A tract of land sufficient to provide 416 farms of 3000 morgen each was allotted to the white men, who resolved to form one community and who elected a Transvaal farmer, Gerrit Jacobus van Niekerk, to be their leader. A comet was visible at the time and the territory ceded to the whites was named Stellaland. A site for a town to be named Vryburg, the seat of government, was selected and building allotments and streets were laid out. At its founding, the new country covered an area of 15,500 square kilometres and was home to an estimated population of 20,500 individuals, 3,000 of whom were of European ancestry. The farms were roughly apportioned until they could be properly surveyed and certificates of ownership were issued which enabled those who did not intend to occupy them personally, to sell their rights. According to Theal[26] "a good class of men from other parts of South Africa then came in and purchased ground, so that Stellaland soon presented the appearance of a perfectly orderly and respectable community."

However, one participant was far from respectable. He was George St Leger Lennox, born into a noble Scottish family and popularly known as Scotty Smith, who was a well-known cattle thief, horse rustler, dealer in illegal diamonds, smuggler and friend of the poor. In his book, FC Metrowich[27] writes that Scotty arrived in South Africa in 1877 to join the

---

26. George McCall Theal, *History of South Africa 1873-1884*, C. Struik, 1964.
27. *Scotty Smith*, Metrowich FC, Cape Town: Books of Africa, 1983.

Frontier Armed and Mounted Police. He is said to have assumed the name of Scotty Smith when he took the papers of a fallen comrade by that name. He was involved in gun-running, general theft, elephant hunting and other hunting activities in Bechuanaland. He was also involved in illegal diamond buying, horse theft and highway robberies. He was caught and sentenced several times for these crimes, but always managed to escape and claimed that no prison could hold him. However, there is no evidence that he was involved in anything untoward while resident in Stellaland.

Van Niekerk proclaimed an independent republic on 7 August 1883 with himself as administrator. A "bestuur" (directorate) was elected, the necessary officials appointed and a new state came into being in South Africa. Then another feud broke out between two Barolong chiefs, Moshete and Montsiwa, and again whites were engaged to assist them. A large number of Boers crossed the border. The British government complained of this but President Kruger was unable to persuade the volunteers to retire.

In Theal's words: "Montsiwa's principal English adviser was a man of good family in England, named Christopher Bethell, who had unfortunately formed a connection with a niece of the chief and who had come to consider himself a member of the clan. It was an extraordinary position for an educated English gentleman to be in, but occasionally such idiosyncrasies, which would be regarded as extravagant in a romance, are met with in real life. Bethell acted as Montsiwa's confidential agent and was believed to have procured not only recruits but large quantities of arms and ammunition at the diamond fields."

Another historian, the late Ilona Somerset[28], wrote that Bethell was a nephew of Colonel Warren, who appointed him to remain at King Montsiwa's place:

---

28. Ilona Somerset, *The Seven Lost Trails And Outdoor Adventures In Eastern Botswana,* unpublished.

Christopher was a scion of the Bethell family, whose estates at Rise and Walton Abbey in the East Riding of Yorkshire had been in the holding of the family since the sixteenth century, and still are. He settled with the Barolong and married a Motswana. Bethell was Cambridge-educated and acted as an unofficial intelligence officer for the Cape Government. His accurate reports alerted the Cape of the anarchy which took place over the next few years.

His counterpart on Moshete's side was Nicolaas Claudius Gey van Pittius, who was elected by the farmers. There ensued a series of skirmishes with some loss of life, burning of huts and seizure of cattle. Montsiwa was eventually held at bay at Mafeking where he and his followers were besieged. He refused to come to terms with his enemies, against the advice of his counsellors and sons, until starvation and disease took a heavy toll with an appalling death rate amongst his followers. Finally he sent for Commandant JP Snyman in the Transvaal to mediate and arrange terms of peace.

As a result of the Convention of Pretoria of October 1882, both chiefs lost a large area of territory which formed a solid block from Ramathlabana to Stellaland. Gey van Pittius immediately issued a proclamation in October 1882 in which he took possession of this tract of land called Rooigrond with the approval of Chief Moshete and named it Land Goosen, the Land of Goshen. Goshen had an estimated population of 17,000, of whom approximately 2000 were of European origin, and covered an area of 10,400 square kilometres. On 6 August 1883 Stellaland and Goshen united to form the United States of Stellaland. Stellaland's laws and constitution were practically identical to those of the South African Republic. It never issued an independent currency, but instead - like all the surrounding states - used the South African pound. In 1884 it printed its own postage stamps, and today these are valuable collectors' items. Van Niekerk's government announced it would levy taxes on all trade going through its territory, which incurred the wrath of Cecil Rhodes as well as the British administration since Stellaland lay on the major trade route to the interior. It was also presumed that the small country could eventually be incorporated into the South African Republic in an effort to circumvent the Pretoria Convention of 1881, which called for an end to Boer expansionism.

Rhodes even asserted that the area was "of such a crucial nature to the Crown that if the territory held by Stellaland remained under Afrikaner control, British presence should fall from the position of a paramount state in South Africa to that of a minor state". At this point the status of the new republic was affected by a not unrelated event. This was the convention signed in London in February 1884 which restored to the South African Republic its position as an independent state. Lord Derby, who had succeeded Kimberley at the Colonial Office, was favourably disposed towards the Transvaal and the wishes of the republican government. He acceded to proposals of the deputation from Pretoria, which was led by President Kruger, except for one point; he could not allow to the trade route to the north to pass out of British control. This was within the new Republic of Stellaland. Kruger wanted the privileges granted in the Sand River Convention of permitting the republic to fix a boundary wherever it chose. He offered to protect British commerce from interference but this was not accepted and he finally had to concede.

The boundary of the republic was only extended to include part of the Korana and Barolong territory which affected the continued existence of Stellaland. In terms of the new convention, the administration, in Derby's words, "was left free to govern the country without interference, and to conduct its diplomatic correspondence and shape its foreign policy, subject only to the requirement that any treaty with a foreign state would not have effect without the approval of the Queen." Cattle rustling continued unabated and in 1884, while Rhodes was negotiating at Rooigrond, Goshenites raided Bankwaketse lands and took large numbers of cattle. The Boers drove their booty through Baralong country, where Montsiwa and his men tried to recover their allies' cattle. In the ensuing skirmish the Baralong lost 100 men, including Christopher Bethell.

Somerset wrote: *While helping to recover the cattle on 31 July 1884, Bethell was wounded and later shot dead by two Boers. Freebooters annexed Montsiwa's territory, hoisted the Republican Flag at Mafikeng and began carving up Montsiwa's lands. This contravention of the London Convention and death of a British official (Bethell) caused the Government to send General Sir Charles Warren as Special Commissioner with a force of 4 000 officers and men. Their directive was "to remove the filibusters from Bechuanaland; to restore order to the territory; to reinstate the natives in these lands; to take such measures as may be necessary to prevent further depredations and, finally , to hold the country until its final destination be known.*

This objective was achieved with little trouble and Bethell's body was exhumed and reinterred at its present place near Mafikeng. The full military funeral was attended by Warren, and the firing party was made up of 200 Inniskilling Dragoons commanded by Captain E G Pennefather, who would command the forces occupying Mashonaland on behalf of Rhodes's British South Africa Company in 1890. A young lieutenant attached to Warren's Staff would become known as the "last great cavalryman" - Field Marshal Viscount Allenby . White, Methuen and Carrington were officers on Warren's staff who would become household names during the Boer War. A balloon corps accompanied the expedition and the ascent made at Mafikeng was the first in Africa.

In December 1884, Major-General Warren issued the following proclamation: *Whereas certain freebooters have invaded and occupied lands in Bechuanaland, belonging to tribes under protection of Her Majesty the Queen; and whereas it is necessary to expel these freebooters by a military force; and whereas these freebooters are connected with and in communication with persons inhabiting the settled districts of South Africa; and whereas some of these freebooters are now living in the district called Stellaland; and whereas the district called Stellaland has a nominal government, administered partly by persons living outside Stellaland, who admit that they have no power to govern Stellaland, and who cannot enter Vryburg, the seat of Government, without the presence of an armed force, and who state that any fresh elections in Stellaland will cause a breach of the peace; and whereas there is no law or real government in Stellaland, and immediate steps are required in aid of law and order, and to avoid the risk of disturbances: military rule is hereby declared in Stellaland, while Her Majesty's troops are in occupation, to be applied so far as is necessary to supplement the existing inadequate machinery of the government; always provided that no responsibility of any nature whatsoever is incurred by Her Majesty's Government with reference to the debt of Stellaland, and the "good-fors" issued by the so-called government, the circumstances of which debt should be inquired into by an adequate court, after consultation with the people of Stellaland, who must take upon themselves all responsibility with regard to all retrospective claims for the administration of government up to the present date. Given under my hand and seal this fourteenth day of February 1885 (Signed) Charles Warren, Her Britannic Majesty's Special Commissioner for Bechuanaland.*

Warren was recalled in September 1885 and appointed a Knight Grand Cross of St Michael and St George (GCMG) on 4 October 1885. The Bechuanaland Field Force, as Warren's force was known, was disbanded. A memorial in stone to the men who lost their lives on the expedition was placed in Cape Town's St George's Cathedral and a similar stone was placed in the Grahamstown Cathedral. The Warren Expedition led to the declaration by Britain of a protectorate over northern Bechuanaland – the Southern part was annexed as a crown colony and incorporated in the

Cape Colony ten years later. Rhodes tried to have the protectorate handed over to his British South Africa Company but was unsuccessful owing to the resistance of the Bechuana chiefs, who petitioned the Queen. He did, however, get control of the eastern strip for the construction of a railway line to Rhodesia. And so, during its short history, Stellaland, though small in size, became a focal point of conflict between the British Empire and the South African Republic, the two major players vying over the territory . After a series of claims and annexations, British fears of Boer expansionism ultimately led to its demise and, among other factors, set the stage for the Anglo Boer War. Whether or not the formal independence of any of these states was ever officially recognised is not entirely clear. In Stellaland's favour, the local chiefs approved of its existence.

The definition of sovereignty in the modern sense was formalised by the Montevideo Convention of 1933: "The state as a person of international law should possess the following qualifications:

(a) a permanent population

(b) a defined territory

(c) a government

(d) a capacity to enter into relations with the other states"

Later still, the European Union declared that "the existence of states is a question of fact, while the recognition by other states is purely declaratory and not a determinative factor of statehood".

De jure recognition by Britain could be implied from a telegram that was erroneously sent by Sir Charles Warren, military commander for British Bechuanaland, to Van Niekerk in which he endorsed Cecil Rhodes's settlement in Stellaland.

Only later did Warren realise that his wording could be interpreted as an acknowledgment of Stellaland's legality, and he tried to deny the message's implications. In February 1884, Great Britain unilaterally declared the area a British protectorate. As a footnote, as recently as 2008 a lobby group called for the area to be re-established as an independent Boer republic. The group claimed to be in possession of 1882 contracts that conferred ownership of the area.

* * *

Governor Wodehouse

Robert Keate

Lt Col Charles Warren

Scotty Smith

Kipling in 1915

8.
Kipling in South Africa (1897)

"South Africa became part of Kipling's life and work for several reasons. His first visit gave him a tantalising glimpse of a sub-continent of great beauty and promise; it was also a place where the great British Empire was still visibly expanding."

(Introduction to Kipling's South Africa, *by Renee Durback, Chameleon Press, Cape Town, 1988.)*

It was in 1891, at the age of 26, that Rudyard Kipling first came to South Africa after a sea voyage on the *Mexican* on the advice of his doctors to restore his ill-health. Twice in India he had broken down from over-work and now "staleness and depression came after a bout of real influenza, when all my Indian microbes joined hands and sang for a month."

He stayed in Simon's Town naval harbour with one Commander Bayly. He was fascinated by the British naval station there.

My Navy Captain introduced me to the Naval society of Simon's Town , where the south-easter blows five days of the week, and the Admiral of the Cape Station lives in splendour, with at least a brace of live turtles harnessed to the end of a little wooden jetty, swimming about until due to be taken up for turtle soup.

He found Cape Town "a sleepy, unkempt little place" but he welcomed the restorative sunshine and the "dry, spiced smell of the land". However, this was no more than a stopover as the voyage continued to Australia, New Zealand, and India (where he was born.)

This winter holiday was to be an annual tradition lasting until 1908. They usually stayed in "The Woolsack", a house on Cecil Rhodes's estate at Groote Schuur (and now a student residence for the University of Cape Town); it was within walking distance of Rhodes's mansion.

After achieving considerable success as a writer, and after his marriage[29] and several years spent in America, Kipling returned to London and was elected to the Athenaeum Club at the age of 32, one of its youngest members. At a dinner on the day of his admission he dined with the editor of *The Times* and two new acquaintances who were soon to play an important part in his life – Sir Alfred Milner and Cecil Rhodes (who was no longer Prime Minister of the Cape but now devoting his energies to the founding of a white settlement in what was to become Rhodesia.) Milner was about to leave England to take up appointment as Governor of the Cape Colony and High Commissioner for South Africa.

Kipling's interest in South Africa was reawakened and again travelled with his family to the Cape "*in the winter of '97, taking the Father with us. There we lived in a boarding house at Wynberg, kept by an Irishwoman, who faithfully followed the instincts of her race and spread miseries and discomforts round her in return for good monies. But the children throve, and the colour, light, and half-oriental manners of the land bound chains round our hearts for years to come*[30]."

With his new status as Poet of the Empire, Kipling was soon on friendly terms with influential politicians of the Cape Colony, including Rhodes, Sir Alfred Milner and Leander Starr Jameson. He described Rhodes as

29.To Carrie, nee Balestier, who he married on 18 January 1892.
30. *Something of Myself: For my Friends Known and Unknown*, Kipling, Rudyard, Macmillan (1937).

"inarticulate as a school-boy of fifteen. Rhodes had a habit of jerking out sudden questions as disconcerting as those of a child—or the Roman Emperor he so much resembled."

Rhodes arranged for Kipling to visit Rhodesia, travelling on the newly-completed railway to Bulawayo. He explored the town on a hired bicycle and was so impressed that he told the Bulawayo correspondent of a London paper:

I have some small knowledge of new towns and the impression I have gathered is that there's no point on which any of them can compare with this city.

On his return journey he stopped off in Johannesburg where he was entertained at a banquet at the Rand Club where he met Percy FitzPatrick, recently released from imprisonment following the abortive Jameson Raid. The two became close friends and Kipling was a frequent guest at Hohenheim where, on hearing tales of his host's experience in the bushveld with his dog, Kipling encouraged him to write them down.

In Kimberley Kipling met Olive Schreiner, who in a letter to her brother wrote that Kipling "was a most lovable little human creature." In Cape Town Kipling admired Rhodes's newly-established fruit farms which he was taken to inspect by the great man himself. But he held no respect for the Dutch. He wrote that "It was against their creed to try and stamp out cattle plagues, to dip their sheep, or to combat locusts, which in a country overwhelmingly pastoral had its drawbacks."

Prior to his return to England he was guest of honour at a farewell dinner at the City Club. Here the editor of the *Cape Times*[31] had asked a 23-year-old private in the army medical corps, who wrote verses modelled on Kipling's "Barrack Room Ballads", to compose a "Welcome to Kipling" poem. The young man's name was Edgar Wallace, and when Kipling met

31. Frederick York St Leger, the authors' great grandfather.

him he extended a friendly warning: "For goodness sake, don't take to literature as a profession. Literature is splendid mistress but a bad wife."

At the outbreak of the Anglo-Boer War, the *Daily Mail* offered Kipling 10 000 pounds to represent the paper as a war correspondent. Kipling declined the offer but agreed to contribute to the war effort with a set of verses. "The Absent-minded Beggar" was put to music by Sir Arthur Sullivan, a tune "guaranteed to pull teeth out of barrel-organs. Anybody could do what they chose with the result, recite, sing, intone or reprint, etc., on condition that they turned in all fees and profits to the main account—'The Absentminded Beggar Fund'—which closed at about a quarter of a million."

Lilly Langtree contributed 100 pounds for the privilege of singing the song on stage.

The song was song and played in music halls, at smoking concerts and drawing-room recitals, and cranked out on barrel organs all over the country. Thousands of copies were rushed through the press. The words were printed on every kind of paper and on silk, satin and linen, and the famous Caton Woodville illustration of a wounded Tommy appeared on tobacco jars, ashtrays, cigarette packs, pillow cases, plates, card holders, jugs and every conceivable china, brass or metal object[32].

On his next visit to South Africa in early 1900, he became a correspondent for *The Friend* newspaper in Bloemfontein, which had been commandeered by Lord Roberts for British troops. He was greeted by HA Gwynne, then Head Correspondent of Reuter's, and Perceval Landon of *The Times*. "You've got to help us edit a paper for the troops," they said. At *The Friend* he also penned an inscription for the Honoured Dead Memorial in Kimberley. Known as the "Siege Memorial", it was described by Dan Jacobson[33] as follows:

32. *Kipling's South Africa*, Renee Durbach, P41.
33. South African-born writer, novelist and critic who became a professor at University College London.

Built out of ruddy-yellow granite brought down from Rhodesia, and complete with a massive cannon manufactured locally during the siege, the Honoured Dead Memorial is an imposing, flat-topped affair, half fortress and half Doric temple. It stands in the middle of a grassed-over traffic circle just outside the grounds of Kimberley Boys' High School, which I attended for a full ten years, so I had ample opportunity to study the memorial and its inscription as I trudged back and forth between school and home. Much later I learned that the words had been composed by Kipling at Rhodes's request. The names of both men had been familiar to me almost as far back as I could remember. In Kimberley – then still a "company town" dominated by De Beers Consolidated Mines.

Kipling enjoyed the attention given to him by all and sundry.

My telegrams were given priority by sweating RE sergeants from all sorts of congested depots. My seat in the train was kept for me by British Bayonets in their shirtsleeves. My small baggage was fought for and servilely carried by Colonial details, who are not normally meek, and I was persona gratissima at certain Wynberg Hospitals where the nurses found I was good for pyjamas. Once I took a bale of them to the wrong nurse (the red capes confused me) and, knowing the matter to be urgent, loudly announced; "Sister, I've got your pyjamas." That one was neither grateful nor very polite.

Kipling came under enemy fire more than once. At the front he learned that the "flower of the British Army" had been ambushed and cut up at a place called "Sanna's Post".

I met an officer who, in the old Indian days, was nicknamed "the Sardine." He was calm, but rather fuzzy as to the outlines of his uniform, which was frayed and ripped by bullets. Yes, there had been trouble where he came from, but he was fuller for the moment of professional admiration. "What was it like? They got us in a donga. Just like going into a theatre. 'Stalls left, dress circle right,' don't you know? We just dropped into the trap, and it was 'Infantry this way, please. Guns to the right, if you please.' Beautiful bit of work! How many did they get of us? About twelve hundred,

I think, and four—maybe six—guns. Expert job they made of it."

He got to know the merits of the commando-leaders. De Wet, with two hundred and fifty men, was to be taken seriously. Smuts (of Cambridge) could handle five hundred but, beyond that, got muddled. "I had the felicity of meeting Smuts as a British General, at the Ritz during the Great War. Meditating on things seen and suffered, he said that being hunted about the veldt on a pony made a man think quickly, and that perhaps Mr. Balfour (as he was then) would have been better for the same experience."

Eventually the "war" petered out on political lines. *Brother Boer—and all ranks called him that—would do everything except die. Our men did not see why they should perish chasing stray commandoes, or festering in block-houses, and there followed a sort of demoralising "handy-pandy" of alternate surrenders complicated by exchange of Army tobacco for Boer brandy which was bad for both sides.*

As mentioned, the Kiplings, after the war, would descend yearly.

... for five or six months from the peace of England to the deeper peace of "The Woolsack," and life under the oak-trees overhanging the patio, where mother-squirrels taught their babies to climb, and in the stillness of hot afternoons the fall of an acorn was almost like a shot. To one side of us was a pine and eucalyptus grove, heavy with mixed scent; in front our garden, where anything one planted out in May became a blossoming bush by December. Behind all tiered the flank of Table Mountain and its copses of silvertrees, flanking scarred ravines. To get to Rhodes' house, "Groote Schuur," one used a path through a ravine set with hydrangeas, which in autumn (England's spring) were one solid packed blue river. To this Paradise we moved each year-end from 1900 to 1907—a complete equipage of governess, maids and children.

When Rhodes was hatching his Scholarship scheme of the Scholarships, he discussed the expense side and it was Kipling's wife who suggested that £250 a year was not enough for scholars who would have to carry themselves through the long intervals of an Oxford "year." So he made it three hundred.

The order of his life at "Groote Schuur" was something like this. The senior guest allotted their rooms to men who wished to "see" him. They did not come except for good reason connected with their work, and they stayed till Rhodes "saw" them, which might be two or three days. His heart compelled him to lie down a good deal on a huge couch on the marble-flagged veranda facing up Table Mountain towards the four-acre patch of hydrangeas, which lay out like lapis-lazuli on the lawns. He would say; 'Well, So-and-so. I see you. What is it?" And the case would be put.

Kipling foresaw the First World War, and tried to alert the nation to the need for preparedness. The Kiplings were to suffer a second bereavement[34] with the death of their son John, at the age of 18, in the Battle of Loos in 1915. But Kipling continued to write, and some of the post-war stories are counted among his finest.

The Kipling Society was founded in 1927 and soon attracted hundreds of members from all over the world. The Kipling Society is for everyone interested in the prose and verse, and

The Kipling story is one of great passion, creativity and entrepreneurial spirit. In 1987, three friends in the fashion capital of the world (Antwerp rules!) decided that women needed high-quality bags that were iconic and chic and feminine and fashionable and not boring! They named the brand Kipling, after the well-known and well-travelled author Rudyard Kipling. Soon, their bags were part of the everyday adventures of women around the world. Today, Kipling mascot monkeys, by far the world`s best-travelled primates, dangle from a full range of handbags, luggage and carry-alls. Trendy yet practical, upscale yet reasonably priced, durable yet daring, Kipling bags are the must-have accessories of over 35 million women in more than 60 countries. That`s some SERIOUS monkey business!

(From the website of Fraser's Luggage)

34. On a visit to the USA in 1899, their daughter Josephine developed pneumonia from which she eventually died.

life and times, of Rudyard Kipling (1865-1936). Best-selling poet, children's author, novelist, supreme master of the short story, he enriched the English language with more memorable quotations than any other writer of his time. This is one of the most active and enduring literary societies in Britain and, as the only one which focuses on Kipling and his place in English Literature, attracts a world-wide membership.

He was also much involved in the work of the Imperial War Graves Commission, and King George V became a personal friend. The Kiplings travelled a great deal, and at the outset of one of their visits, in January 1936, Rudyard died, just three days before his King. He had declined most of the many honours which had been offered him, including a knighthood, the Poet Laureateship, and the Order of Merit, but in 1907 he had accepted the Nobel Prize for Literature.

Rudyard Kipling's reputation grew from phenomenal early critical success to international celebrity, then faded for a time as his conservative views were held by some to be old-fashioned. The balance is now being restored.

More and more people are coming to appreciate his mastery of poetry and prose, and the sheer range of his work. His autobiography *Something of Myself* was written in 1935, the last year of his life and was published posthumously.

The Absent-minded Beggar

WHEN you've shouted "Rule Britannia," when you've sung "God save the Queen,"
When you've finished killing Kruger with your mouth,
Will you kindly drop a shilling in my little tambourine
For a gentleman in khaki ordered South?
He's an absent-minded beggar, and his weaknesses are great—
But we and Paul must take him as we find him—
He is out on active service, wiping something off a slate
And he's left a lot of little things behind him!
Duke's son—cook's son—son of a hundred kings
(Fifty thousand horse and foot going to Table Bay!)
Each of 'em doing his country's work
(and who's to look after their things?)
Pass the hat for your credit's sake,
and pay—pay—pay !

There are girls he married secret, asking no permission to,
For he knew he wouldn't get it if he did.
There is gas and coals and vittles, and the house-rent falling due,
And its more than rather likely there's a kid.
There are girls he's walked with casual. They'll be sorry now he's gone,
For an absent-minded beggar they will find him,
But it ain't the time for sermons with the winter coming on
We must help the girl that Tommy's left behind him!
Cook's son—Duke's son—son of a belted Earl
Son of a Lambeth publican—it's all the same to-day!
Each of 'em doing his country's work
(and who's to look after the girl?)
Pass the hat for your credit's sake,
and pay—pay—pay !

There are families by thousands, far too proud to beg or speak,
And they'll put their sticks and bedding up the spout,
And they'll live on half o' nothing, paid 'em punctual once a week,
'Cause the man that earns the wage is ordered out.
He's an absent-minded beggar, but he heard his country call,
And his reg'rnent didn't need to send to find him!
He chucked his job and joined it—so the job before us all
Is to help the home that Tommy's left behind him!
Duke's job—cook's job—gardener, baronet, groom.
Mews or palace or paper-shop, there's someone gone away!
Each of 'em doing his country's work
(and who's to look after the room?)
Pass the hat for your credit's sake,
and pay—pay—pay !

Let us manage so as, later, we can look him in the face,
And tell him—what he'd very much prefer
That, while he saved the Empire, his employer saved his place,
And his mates (that's you and me) looked out for her.
He's an absent-minded beggar and he may forget it all,
But we do not want his kiddies to remind him
That we sent 'em to the workhouse while their daddy hammered Paul
So we'll help the homes that Tommy left behind him!
Cook's home—Duke's home—home of a millionaire,
(Fifty thousand horse and foot going to Table Bay!)
Each of 'em doing his country's work
(and what have you got to spare?)
Pass the hat for your credit's sake,
and pay—pay—pay !

* * *

The "Absent-Minded Beggar"

Kipling's autobiography

Renee Durbach's book

His American wife, Carrie

The Dead Memorial

The Woolsack

Rhodes courted the Bond

9.
The Rev S J du Toit

Published in English in 1897, S J du Toit's book *Rhodesia Past and Present* had profound implications for the country. It had originally appeared in Dutch in 1895 as *Sambesia, of Salomo's Goudmijnen Bezocht* in 1894. The book made a stirring appeal to English and Afrikaans readers in the Cape to spread civilisation to the north, to excavate the gold of the area and to discover the past through archaeological research.

Du Toit's journey to Rhodesia began in July 1894 when he travelled from Paarl by rail to Vryburg, spending the next three months journeying by ox-cart across Rhodesia. On reaching Umtali he went down to Chimoio and thence by rail and tug to Beira where he caught a boat to Port Elizabeth, completing his journey home by rail. He appears to have represented the Paarl Matabeleland Syndicate which had interests in gold claims and farm land.

The purpose of Du Toit's series of first-hand observer "sketches" was to report progress on Rhodesia - then only four years old - to the South African public. Little escaped his notice and his comments on travel, agricultural opportunities, flora and fauna, the early settlers (with particular reference to Afrikaners), mining prospects, the first urban settlements, African tribal life, and Rhodes's new telegraph and railway, make fascinating reading. His style is vivid and immediate, and his interview with the American scout Burnham of the Shangani Patrol is a rare example of early Rhodesian journalism.

He painted a very favourable picture of the country and, being a man born and bred to the veld, his assessments of the country's natural wealth must have been invaluable to prospective settlers of the day. His speculation on the future development of the railway system and relative merits of the Portuguese and South African ports would also have been of interest.

The book is written to his friends in a series of letters, following former journeys:

We took you first through England, Holland, Germany, Switzerland, and Italy; from there to Egypt and Palestine; thence through Turkey, Austria, France and Belgium, and then via England back to our beloved fatherland. Afterwards we gave you an extensive description of our "Travels through Bible Lands."

He waxes lyrically over the early means of transport:

Where is the African poet, who will worthily sing what the ox and ox-waggon have done for the opening up and development of our country? Poets have extolled in song the merits of the good-tempered camel, that ship of the desert; poets have painted, in beautiful images, the virtues of the fleet and noble horse; the usefulness of the locomotive has often been extolled as high as the heavens, in song; and far be it from me to deny their virtues and usefulness. But who will contradict me when I venture to state, that for the opening and development of South Africa the "slow but sure" ox-waggon has done more than camel, horse, and railway combined?

Du Toit is fulsome in praise of England "God has given us England as a guardian, a more considerate one than Israel found in Pharoah of old."

He drew a distinction between the English Imperial Government and the Englishman in South Africa. He hinted that it might be a good thing if England were defeated by Germany since that would unite English and "Africanders" as a free and independent nation.

Observing the status and power of chiefs in the area to become Bechuanaland, he queries the policy of the Kruger Government.

The method pursued up till now has been to break the power of the great chiefs (naturally not without cause), for instance Kreli, Ketswayo, Sekukuni, Mapoch, Massona, Lobengula, etc. The policy of the Dutch and also of the English in India was to use the influence of the chiefs for their own benefit, by gaining them to their side, and making them virtually servants of the State. Such native chiefs have unlimited influence amongst their people. This policy properly applied can become a factor for good. Suppose the chiefs were allowed to retain their influence over the people, that that influence was confirmed and strengthened, that a location was given to the chief large enough for his people to dwell in, which right he retains as long as he pays taxes and supplies workpeople.

And he showed some pity for the Matabele's plight: their military power having been broken, they were in a worse position than the Mashonas whom they had made their vassals and who now mocked and jeered at them. Their cattle had been confiscated as a "right of war", their mealies taken to feed the horses of their conquerors and their great kraals burnt.

The Rev Stephanus Jacobus du Toit (1847-1911) pioneered the recognition of the Afrikaans language. He also wanted to achieve greater political influence for his movement. In 1881 the Afrikaner Bond, a political party in the Cape Colony, was formed by the union of the Genootskap vir Regte Afrikaners (Society of True Afrikaners) and the Zuidafrikaansche Boeren Beschermings Vereeniging (South African Farmers' Protection Association) of Jan Hendrik Hofmeyr. Instrumental in this union and the resultant founding of the Afrikaner Bond party were a German man named Borckenhagen, who lived in Bloemfontein, and Francis William Reitz (father of the better-known Denys Reitz), who afterwards became the state secretary of the Transvaal Republic.

The Afrikaner Bond aimed to advance Afrikaner interests from the Cape to the Limpopo River. But it was under the inspiration of a leader of a more advanced type in the person of the S J du Toit that the Bond adopted a more hostile stance. Although frequently having a majority in the Cape Parliament, the Afrikaner Bond never governed directly, generally forming coalitions with English-speaking politicians. These included Thomas Scanlon; Cecil John Rhodes, with whom it split after the Jameson Raid; and John X Merriman, the last Prime Minister of the Cape Colony (1908–1910). After Union, in 1910, the Afrikaner Bond ceased to be an independent party and merged with the South African Party in the Union parliament. Du Toit was the founding editor of the first Afrikaans newspaper, *Die Afrikaanse Patriot*, published in the vulgar tongue or *taal*, which he devoted to the dissemination of the most bitter anti-English political doctrines, raising the cry of South African independence under its own flag. In 1882 he had been persuaded to go to the South African Republic (Transvaal) and become director of education.

With General Nicolaas Smit, Du Toit accompanied President Kruger to Britain for the signing of the London Convention on 24 February 1884. This replaced the Pretoria Convention of 1881, which, although it had restored the independence of the Republic, had made this subject to the Republic recognising the suzerainty of Great Britain and abolishing the position of State President. The London Convention restored the office of the State President but still provided for Britain's control of the Republic's foreign policy.

35. Wallace G. Mills Hist. 322 14a Religion and Afrikaner Nationalism.

Meanwhile, his more radical ideas[35] on preserving the Afrikaans language and customs by using the schools as well as some of his other ideas got him into conflict with Kruger's government, and he subsequently resigned, having become very critical of both Kruger and the Republic. *Sambesia*, du Toit's first book, was published after his resignation from the Kruger administration and on his return to Paarl. He may have been disenchanted with the hard line of the Transvaal Afrikaners and he appealed for greater cooperation with the British.

He wrote: *The old Voortrekkers opened the country through the ox-wagon, and the Englishman is now opening it with telegraph and railway line. We are living in a time of transition. What can be more appropriate then to think now what the ox-wagon and what the railway line respectively have done for the opening of our country; to what extent both still mutually need each other and to what extent the Afrikaner Boer and the Englishman have to cooperate under the same Godly mandate to develop our great and good country – the country of the future.*

Du Toit and the Taal movement had tended to be very critical of the British and urged the elimination of what later came to be called the "Imperial Factor" in South Africa, which meant getting rid of any influence or interference from London. However, in the early 1890s he became a friend and supporter of Cecil John Rhodes, with whom he travelled to Rhodesia. As a consequence, before and during the Anglo-Boer War, *Die Afrikaanse Patriot*, under his editorship, supported the British against the Boer republics.

In a sequel to *Sambesia*, du Toit wrote *Die Konginin van Skeba*, the myth of the white Queen of Sheba, purportedly the founder of civilisation in Southern Africa. He appears to use this myth to justify the occupation of Zimbabwe to fulfil the original cultural and economic promise. He was searching for reasons for the collapse of this ancient civilization so that the newly-founded Boer and British colonies would learn from history and not go the same way. He wrote:

Generally, however, it is not difficult to guess what made an end to this blooming colonial settlement here. It has become quite evident, both from the mine-works as well as these ruins, that a higher-developed race, presuming descended from elsewhere, or in any case in living contact with Phoenicia, Egypt and Palestine, were in command and had these works executed by a subjected slave race, which had to be constrained, given all the fortifications. When now the motherland goes under and such a colonial settlement receives no support from there any longer, then it is easily understood that a general uprising of the subjected tribes could put an end to the colonial settlement.

What seemed to convince du Toit of the influence of another race was the aqueducts:

We had so often seen them in Oriental countries, for instance around Damascus. We were firmly convinced that the (local natives) had not made these aqueducts. On our travels through Rhodesia we had seen a hundred places where the ancients had dug gold, where they had lived in their towns, but now it became apparent to us that they had also been agriculturists. Who were these ancients?

Die Koningin van Skeba relates the adventures of the du Toit expedition in two parts. Under the tower of the Zimbabwe Ruins du Toit discovered a so-called parchment scroll in classical Hebrew purporting to having been written by Elihoref, Solomon's scribe and consort of the Queen of Sheba. In the scroll (translated by du Toit) there was an indication that the history of the empire was written on three so-called parchment scrolls discovered beneath Mount Afoer, north-west of where they were at that time. Du Toit translated the scrolls during the day while the rest of the company visited the pyramid-like tombs beneath the mountain. In the evenings the translation was read out to the rest of the party.

In his Preface, du Toit writes:

The reader has probably seldom met with more heterogeneous elements in one single book. Some portions were written in our waggon, some under a tree, on a stone, near an ant-heap, on the brink of a river, on board ship, on the beach, in an old mine, amidst ancient ruins; seldom with the pen, mostly with pencil; sometimes by the glare of a fire, sometimes by the feeble glimmer of a candle in a lantern, mostly with the inconvenience of a traveller in a new country, often in a hurry to avail ourselves of the scanty chances of postal out-stations; mere fleeting impressions, incoherent but fresh, in the shape of letters to friends. On the contrary, other parts were written in my study, in the midst of a library of books on the North, dealing with the old diggings and ruins, the result of much reading and reflection, coupled with my own investigations and experience.

* * *

Rev SJ du Toit

President Kruger

JBM Hertzog

Du Toit's book

DIE

Afrikaanse Patriot.

DEEL 1] SATERDAG, 15 JANUARY, 1876. [No. 1.

"DIE AFRIKAANSE PATRIOT."

"AFRIKAANSE PATRIOT."

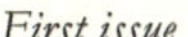

First issue

He believed in the myth

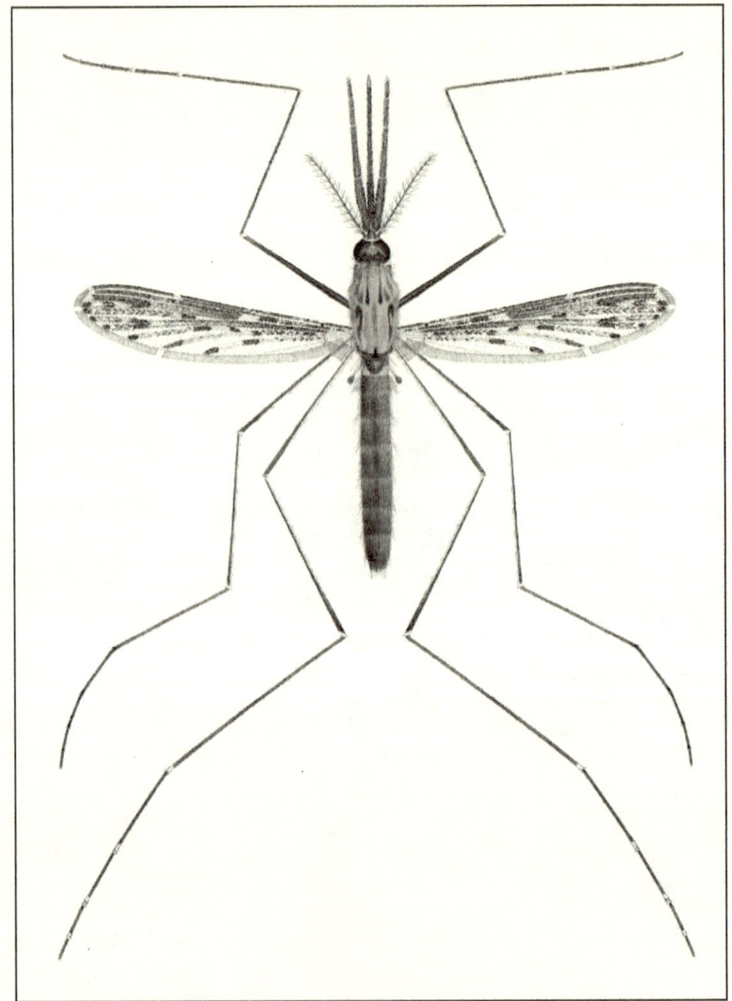

Anopheles funestus

10.

The "Good for Nothing" Mosquito[36]

Swellengrebel and Malaria Control

Professor N H Swellengrebel[37], a world-renowned malariologist from the University of Amsterdam, visited SA in 1930 accompanied by Drs Botha De Meillon and Siegfried Annecke on a tour of the Lowveld areas to investigate the malaria situation. This was reported in a medical journal[38].

The comprehensive report that resulted from this visit recommended the implementation of "species sanitation", this being the specific targeting of malaria vector mosquitoes with control interventions, the indoor spraying with pyrethrum.

Swellengrebel also recommended the establishment of a malaria station in Tzaneen. The SA Institute of Medical Research (SAIMR), at the request of the government, erected this station in 1932 under the leadership of De Meillon for research and Annecke for control. Another station was established in Eshowe, Natal, in 1934. These stations were to provide the basic facilities for De Meillon to demonstrate the utility of indoor spraying with pyrethrum as a highly effective measure against adult, indoor resting anopheline mosquitoes.

Swellengrebel's report to the Department of Public Health of 16 May 1931 recommended making use of malaria-tolerant labour and the promotion of rural sanitation (district nurses of the health visitor type and native malaria assistants.)

He distinguished between "Estate" and "Farm" malaria. The former

---

36. Anopheles - Greek anofelís: good-for-nothing).

37. Professor Nicolaas Hendrik Swellengrebel (1885–1970), had worked for the eradication of malaria in the Netherlands and Indonesia.

38. Malaria in South Africa: 110 years of learning to control the disease, *SA Medical Journal*,Vol 103, No 10 (2013) M Coetzee.

affects the intensive big-scale cultivation of valuable crops and so causes serious financial loss. In farm malaria the fever saps the strength of the white rural population and prevents (or at least seriously interferes with) white settlement of some areas of the Union.

To illustrate the Estate type of malaria Swellengrebel quoted the experiences of a sugar planter on the Natal South Coast who was often on holiday during the off-season of the sugar-growing operations which is when malaria occurs. (He clearly viewed native labour as less-than-human commodity.

When he returns, he might find his native compound depopulated, some having died of fever and the others having returned home. When he tries to get a fresh supply he finds that his usual method of voluntary recruitment fails as his place has got a bad name owing to the prevalence of sickness and death and so he has to apply to the recruiting agencies, to pay capitation fees and to accept what they send him which, more often than not, is nothing more than the dregs of the mines, those disqualified for several reasons. He may deem himself lucky if the fever season is not a late one, otherwise he may see the whole new lot going down with fever within three weeks of their arrival, his cane fields left uncut and the neighbouring sugar-mill having to work half-speed owing to shortage of cane cut. He would not care a bit for malaria if it was not for his cane left uncut and uncrushed.

For the Farm type of malaria he looks at farmer in the Ofcolaco district of the then NE Transvaal. The farmer is living in an area more intensely and continuously malarious than the Natal planter was ever called upon to live in.

Still he has no labour difficulties. What he complains of is that his area has got such a bad name for fever that he cannot get others to come and settle there. He maintains that the place is not such a bad one, but at the same time he admits that it is not an area for women and children to live in, although it is all right for bachelors, and he finds no answer to the question whether he does believe a country where one does not dare to import women and children can ever satisfy the requirements for white settlement.

Swellengrebel identified the *Anopheles funestus* from 20 species of mosquito as being mainly responsible for the transmission of malaria. It breeds in the backwaters of streams and rivers, not, as was widely believed, in swamps and marshes, rainwater tanks, roof gutters and holes in trees. The adult Anopheles is not found in thickets and bush but inside human habitation.

Botha de Meillon (later to become head of the department of Medical Entomology at the SAIMR from 1931 to 1960) undertook the first extensive mosquito surveys of SA covering the Transvaal and Zululand. Having confirmed the insecticidal properties of pyrethrum, he demonstrated the powerful influence that indoor spraying with pyrethrum would have on malaria transmission, this being the forerunner of the World Health Organization's (WHO's) global malaria eradication campaign over 20 years later.

A Pan-African Health Conference was held in Johannesburg in 1936 under the auspices of the Health Organization of the League of Nations. De Meillon's contribution to the conference, outlining controlled experiments carried out in Eshowe, showed that daily spraying with pyrethrum had a 91 per cent reduction in infection.

Dr Fred Soper (from the Rockefeller Foundation) who attended this conference, rejected the concept of vector control by indoor insecticide spraying, stating that for every female anopheline that came indoors there would be hundreds outdoors and out of reach of the insecticide. Soper, however, just a few years later made excellent use of the very same indoor spraying strategy to rid Brazil of *An. gambiae.* He subsequently met

Professor James Gear from the SAIMR at a Rockefeller Institute meeting and asked him to convey his apologies to the South African "malaria officers".

In South Africa, the first well-documented case of the devastating effects of malaria was probably that of the Louis Trichardt trek to Maputo, Mozambique in 1837 - 1838, when 20 of the 53 members of the party died of malaria, including Trichardt's wife. Trichardt himself died of malaria six months later.

It was the scourge of malaria that brought an end to the Boer settlement of Schoemansdal way back in 1886, not the deprivations of the black tribes. It was only after the settlers had left that Chief Latlakter and his Venda warriors burnt the houses and destroyed the crops. It was malaria that brought about the mountain settlement of New Agatha outside present-dayTzaneen, when the wives and families of the gold prospectors in the Murchison Range sought refuge in the cooler climate, even though it was not known then that the cause of the disease was the anopheles mosquito. It is a little known fact that eucalyptus trees were thought to ward off malaria – hence the ubiquitous blue gums that marked every farmhouse in the Lowveld.

The Kruger government sent Dr James Kay to Nylstroom in 1886 to investigate a malaria epidemic there. He reported that malaria was "a term applied to emanations or invisible effluvia from the surface of the earth, chiefly found in marshy lands and supposed to be produced by decaying animal and vegetable matter." (Nylstroom is not in the Lowveld and would not be considered a malaria area.)

Britain's Sir Ronald Ross, an army surgeon working in Secunderabad India, proved in 1897 that malaria is transmitted by mosquitoes, an event now commemorated via World Mosquito Day. Giovanni Battista Grassi, professor of Comparative Anatomy at Rome University, showed that human malaria could only be transmitted by *Anopheles* mosquitoes.

Even today, malaria kills over one million people each year, most of whom are children under five, and almost 90 per cent of whom live in Africa, south of the Sahara. Each year there are more than 300 million clinical cases of malaria, which is five times as many as combined cases of TB, AIDS, measles and leprosy. Malaria is responsible for one out of every four childhood deaths in Africa.

The NH Swellengrebel Laboratory of Tropical Hygiene in the Netherland analyses the causes of tropical diseases and develops methods for the early detection and control of these diseases, including leprosy and tuberculosis.

Swellengrebel receives the Laveran Prize

Botha De Meillon

Siegfried Annecke's book

Elephants in the Zambezi valley

11.
Rory Hensman and his Elephants

Rory Hensman's story, edited by the late John Gordon Davis, is about elephants and Zimbabwe politics and wildlife conservation.

It was about 1974, when the Bush War was starting to hot up, that Rory Hensman was sent on a military patrol down into the Zambesi Valley below Mupata Gorge where the Portuguese outpost of Zumbo is on the north side of the great river, the Rhodesian outpost of Kanyemba on the south side. The orders were to show the flag, look for terrorists and engage them in battle. The patrol totalled 120 men, divided into four platoons. Rory Hensman was section leader of the patrol that went to Chief´s Chitsungu´s part of the country, called Mushumbi Pools. The chief invited them to camp at his kraal. He was a hospitable old man who happened to know Rory Hensman; before he inherited the chieftancy, he had worked on Rory´s father´s farm.

Chief Chitsungu said:

"Nkosi, please come back soon and shoot the wild animals."

They were speaking Chilapalapa, a pidgin of Matabele, Shona, English and Dutch which most people in that part of Africa can speak.

Hensman was taken aback. He was a wildlife conservationist.

"Which animals?"

"All of them. The elephant, the buffalo, the zebra, the warthogs, the hippo, and the baboons. Please shoot them all. And the lions."

"But why?"

Chief Chitsungu said: "Because they eat our crops; our maize and all our vegetables. So we are hungry. And the lions terrorise my people. And the crocodiles, when our wives and children fetch water."

"But do all your people want all the wild animals killed?"

"All. We are angry with the animals. Even when my father was chief he was angry. And his father. They hunted them, like we do, but we do not have guns, only spears and snares."

Rory Hensman said: "And do the other chiefs in this area want the same? Chief Chapota at Kanyemba and Chief Chishungu on the Angwra River? And Chief Chakoma on the Muzengezi River?"

"All. We are all hungry because of the wild animals because they eat our crops."

Hensman thought how to put this. He said:

"Madara, you must not kill your wild animals. Your wild animals are worth a lot of money to you if you use the opportunity correctly."

"But they eat our crops!"

Hensman said: "Chief Chitsungu, I too am a farmer. And my father before me. And my brothers, whom you also remember. We farm well, and we sell our produce, and we make money. Yet we also have many wild animals on our lands. They do not eat our crops and make us go hungry. Why is this?"

"Because you have fences to keep the wild animals out."

"Correct. But it is much more than that. Once we have paid the money to put up the fences, we fertilize that same land year after year, and we irrigate it, so we grow many crops in rotation on the same land, year after year. But you plant your land, grow your crop but you do not fertilize it or irrigate it, so the land gets weak, so the next year you move on to the next piece of land, and you plant that, until that piece is also weak and tired. And so your farmland gets further and further from your kraal, difficult to protect. So what is the solution?"

Chief Chitsungu said: "But we do not have money for fences."

Hensman said: "But you will have the money - from your wild animals! If you conserve them as your asset. You will get the money from the Rhodesian Hunters´ Association, and from the hunters´ associations in America, and England, and Europe, who will gladly pay to come here to enjoy controlled hunting, with licences issued by the government on your behalf - and that money for the licences will be paid to you and your people so you can buy the fences to keep the wild animals out of your farmlands – and money to buy fertilizer, and good seeds. Your crops will increase ten-fold, you will not be hungry. And you will be able to transport your surplus food to the markets in the towns, so you will make more money."

Chief Chitsungu was sceptical.

"Ah! But how can we know this? We cannot plough our land like you white people because we have no cattle to pull the plough because of the tsetse fly which poisons cattle, so our wives have to hoe the hard land." He added: "And we do not have clean water to drink because our wives and children fetch it from the river and the crocodiles and hippo make it muddy near the banks, and they terrorise and kill my people. So you must please shoot the crocodiles and hippo."

Hensman said: "But you will have the money for a tractor if you use your wild animals wisely and let licenced hunters come here to hunt. And you will have money to make boreholes so you have clean water to drink."

"But we do not know how to look after a tractor."

"We will teach you. And to begin with I and my farmer friends will do a joint venture with you, and we will gladly bring our tractors to help you to plough and plant good seeds and fertilize the land. And I am a member of the Rhodesian Hunters´ Association, and all the members will be happy to pay money to buy licences to do government-controlled hunting here, on a sustainable basis so the wild animals can nonetheless reproduce in proper numbers – and this will be supervised by the National Parks and Wildlife Management Department. Madara, the law is that wildlife belongs to the state but the landowner, like you, has the right to use it responsibly and sustainably for his own benefit by government-controlled licensed hunting. Do you understand this law?

Chief Chitsungu wasn´t sure he understood anything but that wildlife were a pest. "Yes," he said.

Rory Hensman continued earnestly: " And the government will send the money from the licences to you so that you can buy fences, and buy more good seed and fertilizers. And the government will send a bulldozer to improve the road from the escarpment down here to the Zambesi so the lorries can come to take your surplus to market so that you can earn money." He ended: "So, Madara, do not kill your wild animals. They are your richest asset."

Chief Chitsungu considered this all overly-optimistic.

"Ah! How can we know the government will do this?"

Hensman said:

"Because the government is very anxious to conserve wildlife, because the animals are part of our nation´s heritage, and the government also wants you to be good farmers and become prosperous. And I have many friends in parliament who will see the good sense in this plan, and I have many friends in the Rhodesian Hunters´ Association, who all have friends in the other hunters´ associations in the rest of the world, and they will all be enthusiastic. " He ended: "So you see, Madara, that it is a good plan, and that you must not kill your wild animals." He smiled, "Do you agree?"

Chief Chitsungu looked doubtful.

"If it will happen. How can a wise man not agree with such a plan if it will happen."

"It will happen, Madara. When this army patrol is over I will return and talk to Chief Chisungu on the Angwa River, and Chief Chapota at Kanyemba, and Chief Chakoma on the Muzengezi, and I am sure they too will agree. And then next year I will come back with my farmer friends, with our tractors and seed and fertilizers and we will plough your lands... And we will plough and plant them close together, near your kraals, so you can protect them more easily."

Chief Chitsungu was not sure he could believe this either. He said: "If you will do this I will be very happy."

When the army stint was over Rory Hensman did go back, as a civilian, and he talked to the other chiefs collectively. They all agreed that it was a good plan. And Parliament and the Wildlife Management Department were enthusiastic, as were the Rhodesian Hunters´ Association and its international affiliates.

That year, when the big rains approached, Rory Hensman returned in a convoy of his white farmer friends, their lorries of seed and fertilizers and their tractors, and they ploughed and planted 300 hectares of the Zambesi Valley. They mounted Lister diesel pumps on rafts in the Zambesi and tributary rivers, and laid irrigation pipes. They could not yet afford to buy the expensive fencing, because revenue had not yet begun to flow from the Hunters´ Association licensing, but they planted pepper hedges and erected brushwood fences to keep the wild animals out.

Everything was going well, if slowly, but the Bush War was now escalating, and times were hard and dangerous for everybody, especially in remote places like the long, vast Zambesi Valley where most of the terrorists crossed into Rhodesia.

When the long Bush War was over, Rory Hensman was demobilised from the army, and he returned to his farm. He was war-weary, and much heartened by Mugabe´s exhortation to white farmers to stay - indeed he was optimistic about Mugabe´s premiership: his televised inauguration speech was moderate, reconciliatory, sensible. And did not the man have seven university degrees, and was he not a devout Catholic? Could not Zimbabwe become like neighbouring Botswana, which was the only well-run, post-independence African country under Sir Seretse Khama, an Oxford university graduate? True, Botswana had only one tribe, the peaceable Tswana, except for the tiny Bushmen clans wandering in the vast Kalahari Desert, but could not Mugabe reconcile the Shona and the Matabele into one harmonious nation?

So, like many a soldier, Rory Hensman returned home after the fighting and killing in the Bush War was over, willing to forgive and forget and farm well for the new Zimbabwe. His farm was called Braeside, 1 200 hectares of good land growing maize, soya beans, cotton, tobacco, wheat and animal feed, all in big irrigated fields around a big rambling thatched farmhouse surrounded by lawns and gardens and exotic trees. He had an airstrip for small aeroplanes, a neat thatched village for his 400 labourers and their families, tobacco-curing barns, stables and paddocks for his polo ponies, and pastures for 200 head of cattle.

Contiguous with Braeside was his brother Gary´s farm, and then his brother Guy´s farm, both similar in size and charm and productivity to Braeside; and beyond were 29 other similar white-owned farms. Between them they built a polo field with a fine thatched grandstand and clubhouse. And between them they had a considerable amount of wildlife on their lands. They had no elephant, but that was about to change.

Rory Hensman was a successful, hard-working farmer, but conservation of Africa´s wildlife was his intense abiding interest; with Africa´s population expanding relentlessly, doubling every twenty years and thus encroaching more and more on the wildlife´s habitat, what chance of survival did fauna have unless the plan he had made for Chief Chitsungu was implemented across the country, indeed across the African continent? So he and his brothers applied to the National Parks and Wildlife Management Department to have their joint farms declared a "Conservancy", which gave it a legally protected status as a game reserve. This was granted. Together with his brothers they bought more wildlife to stock the conservancy, until they had thousands of head of impala, sable, zebra, kudu, waterbuck, inyala, giraffe, bushbuck, warthog, leopard; they had no buffalo or wildebeest because of the danger of foot-and-mouth disease which could spread to their cattle, and any lions that showed up were shot for obvious reasons.

Then Rory Hensman put his "Chief Chitsungu Plan" to the Wildlife Department´s chief officer, who was still a white official. The original Chitsungu project had deteriorated during the Bush War but the department authorised him to revitalise it, and also declared the area a Conservancy, thus becoming a revenue-earning Controlled Hunting Area. Hensman urged the department to make his Chief Chitsungu theory the official policy nationwide wherever suitable, wherever wildlife were a threat to African subsistence farmers; but that would require the approval of Robert Mugabe himself.

Rory Hensman was mighty pleased with the progress he was making for conservation in the new Zimbabwe: he was optimistic that Robert Mugabe would approve of making the Chief Chitsungu theory official policy nationwide. Surely he would see the merit of African betterment, the benefit of African subsistence farmers becoming more productive, harvesting ten times their usual crops on much less land, their new structures and methods financed not by the taxpayer but by the revenue that conservation of wildlife and licensed hunting would earn? Was it not a win-win situation for all, for the African farmer, for the state treasury, for wildlife, for mankind? And would not the rest of Africa begin to follow suit? – would not conservation begin to flourish across the continent where wildlife was presently being decimated, many species threatened with extinction?

That´s where he was when the letter arrived from the Zimbabwe National Parks and Wildlife Management Department. It began: We regret to inform you…

In short, Robert Mugabe had decreed that the revenue earned from hunting licences would go into his Treasury, the fiscus, not to the peasant farmers for fences to protect their crops.

So the Chief Chitsungu project died again: there was no money for fences, seed, fertilizers; the wild animals ate his people´s crops, and again the pumps and irrigation rusted and broke down, and the peasants went hungry. To hell with African betterment, to hell with wildlife, Robert Mugabe wanted the money!

And Rory Hensman was sick at heart with frustration and anger that Mugabe had vetoed his Chief Chitsungu Plan. Instead of African betterment millions of wild animals were going to perish, millions of African farmers would stay impoverished and hungry, the African continent´s people deteriorating, the wildlife continuing to dwindle. The

Zimbabwe Government wanted its new affluent lifestyle financed by the foreign aid poured into its coffers by Great Britain and other countries, money which largely disappeared into offshore bank accounts of Comrade Mugabe and his coterie, his ministers, his police and military generals and his ZANU party officials who had the blood of the Matabele on their hands.

Sick at heart at the failure of his project in Chief Chitsungu´s country, Rory Hensman concentrated on his wildlife conservancy at Braeside, now 60 000 hectares: only the fields of crops were fenced, the rest open bush. They employed 23 game scouts to curtail poaching, and built up their stocks of wildlife by purchasing animals. From time to time they sold surplus animals to zoos and game reserves and ploughed the revenue back into the conservancy.

However, they had no elephant. But that was about to change, and with it Rory Hensman´s life.

Optimistic, the Hensman brothers and other neighbours extended the conservancy to include more nearby farms. And they began buying more species to increase the stock. Meanwhile Hensman returned to the Zambesi Valley with colleagues to Chief Chitsungu´s country. In 1988 the Wildlife Management Department was culling elephants in the Zambesi Valley, in the vast stretch of bush between Mupata Gorge upriver to Kariba. Culling surplus wildlife is a distressing, ugly and unpopular business, but it has to be done from time to time because animals outbreed their environment, causing overcrowding and destruction of the biodiversity, and starvation. Between 1960 and 2000 the elephant population of Zimbabwe rose from 33 000 to 120 000, while the human population during the same period rose from 4 000 000 to 13 000 000. Every game reservation, even the Kruger National Park, has to cull periodically. Aerial counts are made and the necessary number to be killed of any species is estimated and located. Then the Wildlife Department´s sharpshooters go in and wipe out whole groups, adults, pregnant females, adolescents and calves so that there are no traumatised survivors of any particular targeted group left. It is a nauseating business, the air filled with the cacophony of rifle-fire, the thunder of hooves, the stink of blood and blind animal terror.

But nothing is wasted. The farmer upon whose land a cull takes place is entitled to the elephant meat, which is distributed to the African denizens of the area: 88 000 000 kilograms of meat were thus distributed in 28 years. In culls of other species like antelope in government game reserves chartered refrigeration trucks move in to cart the carcases off to the government´s Cold Storage Commission to be skinned, the hides to be turned into leather and floor mats, the meat refrigerated and sold, the horns and hooves to be ground up for gelatine. The ivory is sold at the prevailing internationally-controlled price. Culling is a heart-breaking business, but necessary. And a suitable person who has the land and good intentions can make a contract with the Wildlife Department to buy a young animal orphaned in a cull.

That is what Rory Hensman did when he heard that an elephant cull was about to take place in the Zambesi Valley; he applied to the Wildlife Department to buy two elephant orphans.

He wanted to study them as they grew - and to show that African elephants were valuable because they could be tamed and domesticated like Asian elephants. The calves were trucked, still unconscious, to the government veterinary *boma* in Karoi, beyond the towering Zambesi Valley escarpment. It was a big *boma*, a pen made of stout gum poles: when Rory Hensman arrived there were sixty-eight elephant calves in it, all orphaned in other recent culling operations, some still unconscious, as were Rory´s.

They were winched up onto his truck, and off they set for their new home on Braeside, two hundred kilometres away.

It was late afternoon when they got home. There was great excitement from Rory´s children, African staff and Lindie, his girlfriend, and his African staff: they clustered around the truck, agog. The calves had regained consciousness, their eyes rolling in terror. They were loaded off the truck into a horse stable. Straw bedding had been prepared, green fodder, water, and a mixture of coconut milk and powdered milk in teated plastic bottles.

"See if they´ll take any milk before we untie them. Stroke them, talk softly. Smile. Show them the milk, squirt a little at the trunk-tip so they can smell it."

"Both were females. They were named Miss Elli and Jumbo. We knelt down in the straw, stroked their faces and flanks, crooning softly, 'Hullo, hullo… good elephants…' Their eyes rolled at us, their trunks twitching. I squirted some milk into Miss Ellie´s trunk. Then I pushed the teat into her mouth. She struggled away from it, twisting her head. I shoved it in again, and squirted: she spluttered and coughed; I squeezed the bottle harder, a big jet went into the back of her mouth, and she got the idea – her mouth clamped the teat and she began to guzzle. She guzzled and guzzled, sucking and swallowing. As soon as the first bottle was sucked dry I replaced it with the second. Next to me, Lindie´s little Jumbo was also guzzling."

The elephants each drank about a gallon of the mixture. They were calmer now.

"Now untie their legs. Gently. Talk to them."

Rory and Lindie loosened the ropes. The little elephants scrambled unsteadily to their feet. They turned and staggered to a corner. They bunched together and faced them nervously.

"Well, they now know that we are the purveyors of milk. Tomorrow they´ll want more..."

But they did not leave them alone. The Africans were sent to their village for the night, and Rory´s family sat down in a row in the straw, talking softly to the elephants, and to each other. That night they dossed down in sleeping bags in the stable with them, to reassure them that they meant them no harm, to begin the process of showing them, convincing them that the Hensman family were their new family, their new herd.

*

It did not take long. And Hensman learned that elephants, like dogs, are by nature human-friendly: they are inherently interested in making friends with and attaching themselves to human beings.

"An elephant only wants four things: food security, physical security against enemies, a secure social place within the herd, and leadership. Provide that and an elephant is content, good-natured and malleable."

During the night Hensman awoke to hear the elephants eating the green fodder. They were out of their corner. That was a good sign: they were wary but they had lowered their guard enough to eat. Early next morning they were hungry for milk again. They were offered bottles again. They backed away, ears out, trunks nervously swinging. They could smell the mixture, and they wanted it, but they didn´t trust those outstretched arms.

"We tempted them by squeezing little squirts at them. Oh, they wanted it but did not like those arms. We inched towards them, on our knees, crooning, and they backed away until they were in the corner again. That made it easier for us: we inched forward, still on our knees, talking softly to them, the bottles outstretched. They jostled tighter into the corner, their little trunks waving and fending us off, until we were close enough to push the bottles at their mouths and squirt. That did it – their mouths closed around the teats and they began to suck and guzzle again."

The Hensman family spent most of that day in the stable with them, and they slept with them the next few nights, until the elephants got accustomed to human presence and human smell and the regular ministrations of milk, and being touched.

"We stayed with them and slept with them until they accepted us as part of their lives, their family, therefore their security. After three days of togetherness we let them out of their stable, to show them their new terrain.

"They followed us outside. Perhaps I was already their patriarch? They had never seen buildings before and had only just grown accustomed to the new security of their concrete stable. But we praised them and cajoled them and once outside they immediately followed us closely, trotting beside as we introduced them to the farm outbuildings."

They were shown the extension of the horse stables, the cow sheds, the pastures, the tobacco barns, the office; then they were led into the farmyard, to the house and the beautiful gardens. They were led around the garden, even allowed to uproot a few flowers and snap branches off bushes. Then they were taken into the house. Through the back door into the kitchen, talking to them all the while:

"This is where we cook – smell the food?"

- into the living room

"This is where we sit – you can smell us on the cushions and carpets"

into the bedrooms

"This is where we sleep, you can smell us on the beds."

The little elephants followed through the big house, wide-eyed, trusting, interested, their trunks sniffing at this and that, emptying their bowels from time to time. They met the family puppy, and made friends with him.

The tour finally over, Hensman said to the kids:

"Stay outside with them in the yard. Bring food from their stables. Stay with them, petting them and talking to them. And give them fruit and sugar lumps. Remember they are like puppies and need your attention. In the next few days we´ll take them into the conservancy and show them some of our other animals. And we´ll take them to the staff village to show them that people are okay, that nobody will hurt them…"

Within three weeks the two little elephants were letting the children ride them around the farm. The children loved it, and the elephants enjoyed it. Like puppies, they followed everywhere. Soon Rory began to teach them farm work: riding them whilst herding cattle, dipping cattle, inspecting fences. After six months they began to grow tusks – when they were about two-and-a-half years old. After another year, when they were about five feet tall at the shoulder, Rory began to teach them anti-poaching skills, following the scent of poachers.

The Hensmans were their herd, their family: their food security, their physical security, their social security, their leaders.

In those days getting elephants was not difficult. Numerous farms had unwanted wild elephant which were damaging crops, and usually the farmer intended to shoot the animal unless it was taken off his lands. You could buy an elephant for a few hundred dollars or even get one for nothing, though you had to capture it yourself, which could be expensive and laborious: first you had to get a permit from the Wildlife Department, then you had to track the animal down, and a vet had to dart it with a tranquilizer called M99, then load it by crane onto a heavy-duty vehicle and transport it to its new home. There were specialists who had the necessary equipment, who would do this for you, but they didn´t come cheap. And the elephant had to be adequately accommodated in its new environment.

Without much difficulty Rory Hensman acquired 24 more elephants over next 22 years from farmers. They were all young animals. They quickly settled down to their new terrain and their new herd and established their own hierarchy. Once homed they free-ranged on the conservancy during the day under the surveillance of their grooms, returning to their stables at night. Rory built strong communal stables out of stout telephone poles, bolted together horizontally with large spaces between each pole so the elephant could see out, see and interact with the elephants next door. When the newly captured elephant regained consciousness in his stable he was confused and distressed but seldom did he try to bash his way out: everyone talked to him soothingly, fed him fruit and other delicacies, and as soon as he realised they were not going to hurt him, and that his neighbouring elephants were content, he calmed down. Then his training could begin.

"I teach him to track down poachers, like a bloodhound. Better than a bloodhound. He´ll do it faster, and much more reliably than any trained dog. Elephants are scientifically proven to have a sense of smell fourteen times better than a bloodhound; and a dog´s sense of smell is two thousand times better than a human´s. And an elephant can walk three times as fast as a man with a dog on a leash, therefore cover three times the territory in a given time while expending less than half the energy to do so. And he can do it at night." He added: "I´ll demonstrate this to you in the next day or two. I´ll tell him to track you."

"What do you do with twelve beautiful, loveable trained elephants? Who each eat three hundred pounds of greenery a day. I don´t want to keep them as pets – I want to put them to work, to show the world what wonderful, useful animals they are, so that the world appreciates them and lives in harmony with them. Let wild elephants be wild elephants, like dolphins and whales and birds and other wildlife you´ve seen here today, but for God´s sake let´s also live with them, use their skills to save wildlife by using them as trackers to catch poachers who are destroying Africa´s wildlife – instead of killing elephants, use some of them for agricultural work like those Asian elephants, in forestry, and in tourism – you´ve seen today what wonderful vehicles they are for taking tourists up close to wildlife, much better and closer than doing so in a Land rover. And Africa depends very heavily on wildlife tourism.

"But to enable the tourists to have a more personal, memorable and educational contact with elephants than just an exciting safari ride, I want them to be able to touch and examine the elephants´ body at close quarters, and to see demonstrated what intelligent animals they are, and what remarkable memories they have. I do not approve of teaching animals to do tricks, like circus animals, for the sake of human entertainment. But to educate the public about elephants´ anatomy and to demonstrate their intelligence and memories I have to teach the elephants to lie down flat on command, allow us to examine his mouth, his teeth, tongue, his extravagant eyelashes, his small ear hole, the delicate veins on the back of his huge ears that cool him, his sexual organs, his tail, his feet, his bristly wrinkled hide through which he can feel an ant or a fly. And to demonstrate his remarkable memory I have had to teach him a few circus-type tricks that would really impress his audience so much that they would talk about it after they left."

"African elephants and African man make unhappy bedfellows: both species multiply so rapidly that they invade each other's habitat. And both species are wasteful: elephants eat three hundred pounds of vegetation per day, 5 per cent of their bodyweight, but they destroy 10 times that, fairly stripping the land in their path – Africans are subsistence farmers who plant a patch for themselves until it is exhausted, then move on to another patch. But Africans multiply faster than elephants because they have multiple wives, and their gestation period is only nine months, and the human female is fertile every month for several consecutive days: the elephant female is only fertile for a few hours once every five years and her gestation period is twenty-two months. It may not be Politically Correct to say so, but it does follow, both zoologically and environmentally, that the human species is more responsible for conflict between man and beast over land than the elephant. Before the white man came two hundred years ago there were two hundred million Africans: now there are two billion. Before the white man came with his guns and medicines and Law and Order and hunger for ivory the elephants had access to almost 100 per cent of the land: now the elephant has access to only 1.7 per cent in South Africa. And still the human species demands more of the land, what little that is left to the elephant. It inexorably follows that soon, within your children´s lifetime, there will be no land left for those elephants outside a few wildlife reserves like the Kruger National Park. And even enormous reserves like Kruger have to cull them, shoot thousands every year because there is not enough land. There are too many people. Soon Man will surely eat up and destroy the continent of Africa unless we implement the Chief Chitsungu Theory."

Rory Hensman

John Gordon Davis

Robert Mugabe

The Spekboom River, which rises in the Mount Anderson water catchment area, joins the Waterval River and flows in a northerly direction to the confluence with the Steelpoort River, north-west of Burgersfort. It is worth recording the background to the historic bridge over this river which was erected in 1897 further down-stream on the farm "Potloodspruit", a construction far ahead of its time. This arched steel structure with a steel deck spans 30m with a passage width of 7m. The sub-structure was built of hard "blue-stone". Two stone pillars originally supported the steel deck. During the Anglo-Boer war (1899-1902), after the British had occupied Lydenburg in 1900, part of the steel deck was deliberately damaged by the Boer Commandos under General Ben Viljoen to hinder them reaching Pilgrims Rest where he had his headquarters. In 1903 it was replaced with stone by and renamed the Spekboom Bridge. It was declared a national monument in 1973.

12.
Coming Home to Roost
Doug Starling

Doug's life has been a roller-coaster which has whirled him hither and thither. Now he is becalmed in a quiet stretch of a beautiful river in the Drakensberg.

Who better to describe it than Robert Kirby:

If a prize were awarded for imagination and the will to bring dreams to reality, it should be given to a man named Doug Starling. He acquired a piece of land about an hour's drive from Lydenburg. Through it gurgled four kilometres of a surly, unpromising stream, called the Spekboom, which in mid-summer was no more than the gentlest of flows and at best only a reasonable piece of water. The valley through which this stretch of the Spekboom runs is exquisitely beautiful. High rocky krantzes rise abruptly from some pools, whereas the banks of others are wide and flat. Here and there are the crumbling remains of the gold rush days, the ruins of old shacks, long-forgotten tunnels into the mountains, shored up sections of the river bank where once the hopeful panned. The name of the place is Highland Run.[39]

Robert Kirby is perhaps better known as a satirist and playwright of earlier days, but his love of fly-fishing and his description of this wonderful sport at Highland Run will endear him to me for ever. He goes on to say:

39. Andrew Levy,The Magic Valley, Freshwater Fish and Fishing in Africa, Nelson, 1963.

Today this little river boasts some of the most delightful angling imaginable. By the most intelligent use of weirs, the stream had been fashioned into a series of long runs and ponds, with such subtlety that often it is impossible to decide whether a particular run or small waterfall is the work of nature or man.

Robert Kirby conjures up such a wonderful vision of this beloved stretch of water. Starling designed these runs and ponds and developed his own method of constructing rapids rather than artificial weirs made from concrete blocks. These rapids were formed by piling rocks together to slow the water flow, still allowing the stream to flow underneath. The result was the crab population and the aquatic water life continued, and when summer rains came the fish could move up and over the rapids. A section of the river was specifically designed for the dry-fly, half a kilometre of lively runs and pauses emptying into a sedate pool. Other sections have been designed for the deep-sunken fly, some easy to reach, some requiring either the technique to produce a thirty-metre cast or the ability to traverse a rock wall. Those able to tear themselves away from the five kilometres of rapids, riffles, runs, glides and pools can hike and bike in the Reserve, in the company of over a hundred species of Highveld avifauna. Highland Run is also home to a wide variety of flora and fauna, including many species of antelope and the elusive leopard.

Doug confesses that he had accurately assessed the hidden potential of the then ragged stream from the air and, ignoring the dire warnings of others, he set about creating a dream fishery. He brought to bear his in-depth experience of irrigation technique, his innovative theories and newly-acquired love of fishing. Through hard work and determination his dream became a reality, and the result is possibly the finest mountain stream fishery in the whole of Africa, a stream of great beauty from what was once an almost unapproachable trickle.

Way back in the 1970s Doug was a member of the Three Falls syndicate, near Lydenburg, where the trout fishing is comparable to the best in South Africa. As a sugar farmer living in a very hot climate in Malelane, Doug emulated the practice followed by the average farmer in Natal: a beach cottage and a place in the Berg. His beach cottage came to an end with the Mozambique War but he did the fishing at Three Falls.

He was bitten by the fly-fishing bug and decided to look around for a suitable property where he could set up his own fishing syndicate. One of the guests at Three Falls had arrived in a light twin-engine aircraft, so Doug persuaded the pilot to fly him up the Spekboom valley. He was accompanied by Neils Rosenvelt and Andrew Levy. Andrew is one of the country's leading labour relations consultants and also writes on trout fishing. His description of the place sums it up better than most:

"The Spekboom is a beautiful stream set amidst the wildest of rugged scenery. In places the rock-crowned slopes rise almost sheer from the river banks; in others, where the river curves and twists with the valley floor, there are krantz pools of deep green water [40]."

He goes on to praise the Spekboom as one of the finest trout streams anywhere, on par with many famous international streams, and that those who fish it are privileged indeed.

To quote Andrew Levy again:

"A minimum of small wild trout have given way to a bounty of superb specimen fish, including trophy-sized fish big enough for even the most finicky of specimen hunters. Today the crystal clear water glides over gravel breeding redds, drops into dark pools with secret lies of huge trout, and runs in richly oxygenating gurgles over boulder strewn riffles and runs. This stream is a fisherman's pot `o gold. Everywhere, the stream-reading

40. Fly-Fishing in Southern Africa, *Robert Brandon-Kirby, Struik Winchester, Cape Town, 1993, P113.*

fisherman will find lies and holding spots. The spectrum of fishing is complete, offering everything from fast water to almost still slowly eddying pools."

There is another quote which reads:

"There are some in whose company you might not care to spend every day, but I doubt that you would be moved to homicide. I would guess that the fairly obvious reason for this is that if we all choose to share in a large degree the mild eccentricity and freedom of spirit that marks the true fly fisher, then we are all going to have something in common."

Then there is the quote in *The Compleat Angler*, by Izak Walton, first published in 1653:

"God never did make a more calm, quiet, innocent recreation than angling."

But to get back to Doug's story: their first port of call was the farm "Finsbury". (Incidentally, Finsbury is the name of a district in Islington, London, and also the name of a station on the London Underground.) The owner wasn't interested in selling but suggested they try the neighbouring farm, a 400-hectare portion of Nooitgedacht. This was Doug's bonanza! Yes, the owner wanted to sell and move to the Cape. (Maybe he wanted to settle at Nooitgedacht wine estate near Stellenbosch!) In the event Doug bought it for R125 000, and gave it the name of Highland Run. There was a good reason for the land in that area being undeveloped, untouched and unspoiled. It was still designated as mining land and there were mining claims all over the place. There were even people actively engaged in mining, some of whom Doug knew, including a distant relative who thought Doug was being very unpleasant for kicking him off.

Starling also learned that the Spekboom valley was officially proclaimed a gold field on 14 May 1873. For the first decade after the proclamation some 3 000 prospectors thronged the area. Their mining activities centred mainly on recovering alluvial gold from the streams with sluice-boxes and cradles. This method was used to mine gold dust and gold nuggets as well.

Heavy boulders had to be removed to get to the gold which lay in the soft ground underneath them. This was done by digging a pit close to the rock, which was then pushed over, but sometimes it rolled through the pit and crashed on to the workers below. As has been mentioned, evidence of this activity can still be seen today.

"We have picked up old cocoa pans and old railway lines – there were about 3 000 people mining in our valley between 1870 and 1880, prior to Barberton and Pilgrim's Rest. They picked up nuggets of gold but never found a reef. Apart from leaving gullies and trenches, those early miners succeeded in totally eliminating the indigenous fish in the valley, poisoned by cyanide. We cannot be accused of wiping out the local fish by introducing trout, but that issue is still continuing today."

Doug's idea was to form a fly-fishing club. He promoted the venture via regular lunches at the Inanda Club in Johannesburg where he was a member from his polo-playing days. He had always felt very much at home at the Inanda Club, which was founded in 1934 with the amalgamation of the Johannesburg Polo Club and the Rand Hunt Club and whose early members had closer links with Britain. Many, if they had not been born there, had been educated at English public schools or at "Oxbridge."

He invited friends and colleagues to his Inanda Club luncheons with a view to sign them up as members of Highland Run fly-fishing syndicate. An annual fee would entitle them to book weekends at his farm. The fishing was good and it was very popular. Downstream was a hatchery, which allowed Doug to do the initial stocking up of his stream to set the whole thing going.

One very pompous fellow virtually invited himself. Doug remembers him arriving in a hired yellow Rolls Royce, promptly berating Doug for not running the show as he had, at Three Falls farm. He was actually covering himself as he had not paid his club membership for four years. He stood up at the lunch table, threw down his napkin, said he was resigning and stormed out, whereupon there was a clamour from most of the guests who wanted his membership, and they all joined.

Doug wanted to secure the water upstream to ensure it was in safe hands. This was absolutely essential since any mining activity could wreck the whole scheme. So he went back to Finsbury, where the owner by this time did want to sell his farm, together with a large house on it, at very reasonable price, and everything fell into place. The bubbling runs of the Whiskey Spruit, Steenkamp's Kloof and Kliprots streams meander through the farm, combining to form the Spekboom River.

He couldn't buy Finsbury on his own account, having exhausted his resources with the purchase of Highland Run, so he had to find outside finance. In looking at other syndicates he met GT Ferreira and Laurie Dippenaar from Rand Merchant Bank. GT caught a good fish and decided that he would take an interest in this property, and so they backed Doug, and Rand Merchant Bank developed the Finsbury project. The original plan was for 12 homesteads but RMB's property developer adviser thought it should be double that number.

Finsbury is 2 000 hectares in extent and later the syndicate bought more land to bring the total area up to 3 000 hectares. Finsbury not only caters for those brandishing fishing rods! Its walks and hiking trails in fresh mountain air with over 40 km of breath-taking scenery, is rich in bird and wildlife. Big-name fishing gurus from the US and Britain have been trekking over to see what South African fishing is all about. And so have the Japanese — 20 fishermen, most of whom do their fishing on the lawn!

Japan lacks fishing rivers, so the Japanese must travel to put the casting they have practised to a real test. Their delight at the Spekboom was intense.

In 1985 there appeared to be renewed interest in mining at Finsbury. Starling found out, almost by accident, that many of the claims were owned by an international company with headquarters in Canada. He also discovered that they were breaking the law in that the United Nations had, at that stage, placed sanctions on any new investments in South Africa. Doug travelled to Canada with a view to buying their claims. The CEO was highly incensed when Doug suggested that the Toronto newspapers might be interested in a story and accused Doug of trying to blackmail them. Nevertheless they were obliged to sell and as a consequence Doug bought not just the many mining claims, but the whole company, Translyden, which he still has as a shell. The price of R200 000 was a give-away in those days, especially as the company held all the claims from Mount Sheba through to just outside Lydenburg. Doug thought he had acquired only the claims on Finsbury!

The trout industry started back in 1912 when J Gurr, the postmaster of Lydenburg, unexpectedly caught a fish that looked like a trout in the Dorps River. The first trout fingerlings were released in 1916 into a few local streams from hatcheries in the mountains of the Cape winelands. FC Braun, the local watchmaker and jeweller, took over the job of stocking the streams with trout, after Gurr's departure from town. Braun apparently had transported fish in milk cans with ice from a hatchery in Natal and released them in the mountain streams. When I bought Highland Run, there were trout up to two or three pounds in the river. Strangely enough the fish and the Cape clawless otter, which is mainly a Crab-eater, seemed to exist in harmony.

The Canadian company imposed a condition that their identity would not be disclosed. This was an interesting exercise altogether, the farmer versus the mining giant, a company larger than Anglo American! Anglo incidentally had some claims themselves which they gave up.

There was still mining going on and Doug saw people, including the Minister of Mines, visiting the area. He realised he had to stop this before it went too far. This is a pristine area as far as nature conservation is concerned with many rare plant species.

In 1990 Mike Rattray, who is a relation of Doug's by marriage, exercised options on 8 000 hectares of land in the Lydenburg district, and the consolidation of these properties led to the formation and proclamation of the Mount Anderson Water Catchment Reserve in 1993. This reserve safeguards the entire river system and represents the contribution to fairly extensive water conservation – and the simultaneous protection of indigenous highveld fauna and flora.

Michael Rattray's first action after this land acquisition was the removal of all exotic livestock. The use of these former summer grazing areas for sheep and cattle had denuded the flora, and in turn damaged the catchment areas of the five rivers that rise on the property. Overgrazing of the grass cover had seriously affected the water-retaining sponges, but the simple removal of bulk indiscriminate grazers restored the rivers to produce a strong year-round flow. A comprehensive exotic plant eradication programme was also initiated which saw the removal of all plants and trees not indigenous to the area, including eucalyptus, wattle, and pine.

Mike is indeed a crusader for water conservation. His family had owned MalaMala Game Reserve, adjacent to the Kruger National Park, since 1964. During this time he witnessed, with concern, the river levels dropping lower each year. In the winter of 1982 the perennial Sand River on MalaMala stopped flowing for the first time in living memory, an unfortunate state of affairs which applies to most of rivers in the Kruger

Park. The continual decline of in-stream flows has a potentially disastrous effect on wildlife biodiversity, and the protection of water resources is imperative to ensure the sustainability of wildlife, and to encourage an ongoing increase in tourism.

A committee of neighbouring landowners, all of whom have experienced the benefits of water conservation, constitutes the Mount Anderson Water Catchment Reserve, with Michael Rattray as the driving force behind its foundation. These properties are already a proclaimed nature reserve. Much of the revenue generated by this area is as a result of tourism, with the majority of income derived from trout-fishing and its associated industry.

The property owners have had their inclusion in the Mount Anderson Catchment Nature Reserve placed on their title deeds to protect them from any exploitation, mining activity or land claims. This gives them the same status as the Kruger National Park. Doug's dream is that the same pattern should be followed on all the water catchment areas along the Berg.

Andrew Levy

Barry Davison

Charles Fiddian-Green

Echo Caves near Ohrigstad

13.
Albert Machimana

Albert Machimana was a fine teacher, a senior inspector of schools (at the time this was a discipline to ensure teachers were in school, in class and teaching) and latterly a translator of educational material for a major publishing house. For all his talent and education, he was a humble man who could well be a role-model for any young South African.

Albert's father, Michael Moyo, was a Shona from the then Rhodesia, and he moved to South Africa in about 1940 to work at Letaba Estates, a major citrus producer near Tzaneen in Limpopo Province. He married Helena Mundavadzi Machimana, a Tsonga woman from the nearby township then known as Banana Siding. And it was at Letaba Estate's staff village, known as Dudukwela, that Albert was born in 1944.

Letaba Estates, established in 1919, was originally laid out as a potential settlement scheme for ex-soldiers to learn the principles of citrus culture on the job. In those days the area was pretty wild, even after the scrub had been cleared. Sable antelope, kudu and impala were to be found in the thick bush, and crocodiles and hippos infested the Letaba River. Some 2000 acres of ground were cleared and 400 plots of five acres each were laid out, each plot planted with 500 citrus trees. But the enterprise failed to attract sufficient interest and the company was taken over by the mighty Schlesinger organisation some years later. It is still a model citrus estate which exports fruit throughout the world and produces orange-juice concentrate and cattle food from the pulp and skins.

Conditions were not pleasant when Albert's father was taken on as a labourer. The weather was unbearably hot and malaria was a constant threat, especially to families with young children. Newcomers were warned to watch out for the most dangerous of all South African snakes, the black mamba, which was prevalent, and also to be wary of crocodiles in the river.

Michael Moyo was a devout Christian and had adopted the Catholic faith before he left his home country. Young Albert grew up in this religious environment. A Catholic priest from Magoebaskloof used to visit the village at Letaba Estates to minister to the family. Soon after, the Holy Family Mission was established by Irish Catholics at Ofcolaco, which was much closer to Letaba, and a priest from this mission took over the regular visits,

Ofcolaco is an acronym of the Officers' Colonial Land Company, an enterprise formed by a group of retired British Regular and Indian army officers who pooled their resources and settled in this area in the early 1920s. Today this would seem a crazy venture by a group of young idealists who knew nothing about farming, but at the time it was a serious undertaking. The original shareholders were all commissioned officers who had taken part in the First World War.

At the start of the enterprise an area of 123 000ha was acquired at the foot of the Northern Drakensberg in the Thabina area. As time went by, the land holdings were reduced and finally bought out by a handful of enterprising farmers. And it was alongside one of these farms that the Holy Family Mission was founded. This a Catholic institution operated by the Jesuit Order. (The mission closed some years later and became the Holy Family Care Centre, catering for the needs of the sick and vulnerable, especially orphaned children with HIV and AIDS. An International community of sisters, The Daughters of the Lady of the Sacred Heart, administer the Centre which is non-denominational.)

Part of the mission's vision was a primary school and to encourage children to attend, tuition and boarding fees were waived. Albert, then seven years old, and his brother Lucas, only five, were among the first intake. Soon their parents were able to move from Letaba Estates to the mission, where Albert's father obtained employment as a general worker.

After school the children worked on a nearby farm, belonging to a Mr Granville, picking fruit. The agreement between the farmer and the mission was that, in place of remuneration, the children would return in the late afternoon with wheelbarrows laden with papaws. Child labour? Young Albert shakes his head at the memory. "It was fun," he said. "We enjoyed the work."

The school catered for children up to the then standard five, and when Albert passed this stage the priest arranged for him to attend a Government school in Duiwelskloof (now Modjadjiskloof), and he boarded with Father Murphy at the Catholic Mission there. He was only there for a year before he was sent up to Pietersburg (now Polokwane) to attend Pax High School for boys which, together with the Motsi Maria High School for girls, was run by the Catholics.

Albert was encouraged to prepare for the priesthood which necessitated the study of Latin, and he was the first scholar to take Latin lessons with Father Rupert Maluleke. By the time young Machimana had passed his Junior Certificate in 1962 he realised that, as attractive to him was the career as a priest, he had to consider his obligations to his family – he was one of eight siblings and none of them had had the benefit of a proper education.

He discussed the matter with Father Rupert, who agreed that the young man had taken the right decision and a change of direction was required. "But," he said, "You must go on with Latin. And," he added, "there is the question of school fees now that you are no longer on a religious bursary."

Albert discussed this with his parents during the holiday, and his mother visited the general dealership at Ofcolaco to enquire after a temporary job for her son. She was told to send the lad in for an interview. Now the owner of the shop was Paddy Porter, son of the legendary Jimmy Porter of Leydsdorp whose hotel was the watering hole of the horde of prospectors who converged on the goldfields there in the 1890s.

When Albert presented himself for the interview the following day, Paddy asked him one question: "Do you pinch?" On being assured that the answer was in the negative, he was taken on. From then on, Albert worked as a counter hand in Paddy's shop. Not only did his new benefactor pay his school fees, but there was no question of repayment until after the completion of his studies.

In 1963 Albert was transferred to the Porter's general dealership in Leydsdorp. At the end of the holidays, when stock-taking was done, there was a discrepancy of only 5 cents! Albert had certainly earned the trust of his employer.

It was at this stage that the Nationalist Government began flexing its muscles in terms of the recently adopted apartheid philosophy. An announcement was made to the effect that foreign workers would be repatriated to their home countries – Rhodesia, Malawi, Botswana and Zambia. By then Michael Moyo had left the mission and was working on a nearby farm owned by a Mr Slabbert. He called the family together to consider their position. After discussion it was agreed that they should adopt the surname of their mother, and henceforth they were known as Machimana.

Meanwhile Albert continued his studies with diligence. In 1964 he wrote the Joint Matriculation Board examination. Back at Ofcolaco, this time working during his vacation as a petrol attendant at Paddy Porter's filling station, he waited for his results. Paddy walked to the local post office where Mrs Venter, the postmistress, handed him the official envelope.

"He has passed," she told Paddy.

"How do you know?" he enquired.

"If the envelope is thick, it means that there are supplementary papers to write. This one is thin," she said.

And indeed, that was the case. Albert had achieved an M2.

Paddy put him in his bakkie. "We are going to Leydsdorp to celebrate." And to Albert's dismay he was taken into the hotel bar, which was filled with a crowd of khaki-clad whites. "I was a Bantu," he recalled later. "What would happen to me?"

He need not have worried. Paddy banged on the counter and said: "Of all the young people from Ofcolaco who wrote matric this year, Albert here achieved the best results."

And everyone in the bar raised his glass and cheered.

"This was my first glass of whiskey," Albert admitted later. He was reluctant to mention the names of the other matric writers from the area, the Noel brothers, young Luther. That would be rubbing salt into their wounds!

Later, back at his office in Ofcolaco, Paddy summoned Albert. "I have applied for a scholarship for you, to study medicine at Edinburgh University. What do you say?"

Albert was dumbstruck. A chance to attend a world-class university! To study to become a doctor! But seven years away from home, and what would become of my family?

"No," he told Paddy. "I can't take this. I'm sorry. I have to look after my family"

"What do you want to do?"

"I want to study for a two-year diploma in teaching and teach my brothers and sisters."

"Right," said Paddy. "I will arrange payment of your fees at the University of the North. But you must first take a BA degree and then you can do your diploma."

True as his word, Paddy personally visited the Vice-Chancellor, Prof Potgieter, and after satisfying him of Albert's credentials, arranged for a bursary from the Shell Company. (Incidentally Potgieter later became the first Commissioner-General of the Bantu Homeland of Gazankulu.)

Thus in 1965 Albert started his studies at Turfloop, as the University was popularly known. During his initial interview with the Senate his previous study of Latin was revealed. A Belgian, Professor Delport, was delighted. "You must continue with this. I will be your tutor." Albert agreed, and as he was the only student to take Latin, tutorials were held in the Professor's study. Often these extended to four periods and Albert would fall asleep. His tutor would smoke his pipe until Albert would awake with a start. "Are you ready to go on?" he would be asked, much to Albert's embarrassment.

Albert was a conscientious learner and in three years he achieved his Bachelor of Arts degree, majoring in Northern Sotho and Psychology (with a C symbol for Latin). This was followed by two years of study for his UED (University Education Diploma).

For his graduation in 1968, Paddy Porter bought his graduation regalia and Father Broderick brought his parents to attend the ceremony.

Albert successfully applied for a teaching post at Phangasasa High School at near Burgersdorp, and before taking up his post asked Paddy how he could repay the money that had been spent on his behalf.

"You owe me nothing," was the response. "Just educate your siblings."

When Albert reported for teaching duties at the start of the academic year, the principal, Norman Shipalana, asked him to teach Afrikaans at the school, although his experience with the Afrikaans professor at University had been rather unpleasant. He had confronted the professor after receiving less than 50 per cent in two tests, wanting to know why his marks were so low when he had answered the questions to the best of his ability. "Write what is in the book," he was told. So much for independent thought!

Hearing of his prowess in Latin, Headmaster Shipalana also asked him to teach Latin to his two children after hours. Albert was happy to do this, and after three years Margaret and Eric Shipalana achieved A and B symbols respectively.

It was at Phangasas that Albert fell in love with Sylvia, the homecraft teacher. They were soon married and she proved to be his lifelong companion.

The Education Department recognised the talents of this young teacher, and in 1973 Albert was transferred on promotion to Dumela High School in Julesburg, as Principal. This was a new school and started with only one classroom, loaned by the adjacent Rhulanni Primary, the principal of which was the legendary Mr Mashele.

Apart from his administrative duties he taught general science with the aid of a mobile laboratory, and English. He found that his young students were critical thinkers and asked insightful questions. "I was inspired by this, and I became a learner as well as a teacher; I had to prepare myself before classes,"

Tito Mboweni, past Governor of the Reserve Bank of South Africa, recalls the time when he was taught by Albert Machimani.

"Two examples of his creative teaching can be mentioned here, just to illustrate what a remarkable inspiration he was to us. One of the prescribed books was John Buchan's *Thirty Nine Steps*. This is a thriller, set in Scotland. Machimana happened to know that Sister Benedicta, a nun at a Catholic mission at a village called London close to the Olifants River, had studied Buchan's literary career and knew the setting of this, his most famous novel. So he took the whole class to spend a full day's session with her.

"The other happened in a biology class. He told us to bring plastic packets, known as 'Checkers', to school and these were placed over plants is the school gardens. The next day he took us out to collect the packets, which were naturally moist inside, and this was the basis of his lecture on transpiration. Incidentally, this happened to coincide with a visit by a school inspector, one Mr Dirk Scholz. He sat at the back of the class as an observer. Sometime later, Machimana received a telephone call from the regional office at Ritavi to enquire about the inspector's visit. Apparently he had returned with a glowing report of the teaching skills shown in this incident.

Mboweni related another example which made a lasting impression on his understanding of human life. He took the class on a day's outing to the Echo Caves near Ohrigstad in Mpumalanga, a vast underground limestone grotto which winds beneath the mountain. But it was the nearby Museum of Man, located in an ancient cavern, which gripped his youthful imagination so vividly. This was inhabited by the San people some 85 000 years ago. Paintings on the cave walls include a man on a horse, giraffe, warthog, ostrich and trees. Archaeologists from the Universities of Pretoria and the Witwatersrand have excavated the floor of the cave where these people slept on warm ash covered by animal skins. Layers of this ash have been carefully uncovered to reveal traces of this ancient civilisation. Fossilised animal bones, roots and leaves go back 3-million years.

Stone Age people have also inhabited this site, evidenced by beads and bracelets fashioned from ostrich shells. Relics of iron smelting have also been found here in the form of assegai heads, axes and picks.

At the back of the cave a giant "Pillar of Atlas" appears to hold up the roof. It is in fact an ancient stalactite from the top meeting its opposite-number stalagmite from the floor. An excavation at the side of the cave was used as an ancient refrigerator to store meat, cooled by the constant dripping of water.

Many thousands of years later the cave was occupied by the Bapedi. It was used as a hide-out from the warring Swazis and also to hold ritual ceremonies. These inhabitants were early farmers who grew grain, hence their winnowing baskets, grinding stones, jugs for drinking beer and clay pots for water.

Then came the Voortrekkers in the 1870s en route to the Lowveld. They too left remnants of their brief stay – several tools and a wagon wheel.

"What a way to learn the history of one's people! There, before our eyes, was evidence of the past hundreds of generations," Mboweni concluded.

Albert's Graduation

Jimmy Porter's grave

Typical Mashatu scene

14.

The Tuli Block

(Extract from the writings of the late Ilona Somerset[41] circa 1994)

* * *

In the 19th century, the Tuli area was renowned for teeming game, but tsetse fly deterred most hunters. During the 1860s and 70s, Finaughty, Selous, Viljoen, Jacobs, van Rooyen, Hartley and others slaughtered the elephant until only a small herd remained at the confluence of the Shashe and Limpopo Rivers. The Prime Minister of South Africa, Jan Smuts, wrote to the Resident Commissioner in 1941, proposing that the area be proclaimed a game reserve, as South Africa had already declared the land on its side a game reserve. Sir Charles Arden-Clarke, the Resident Commissioner, relayed the proposal to the Bangwato Regent Tshekedi Khama, who rejected the idea as elephant were protected in the area by law. By 1956 the elephant population had grown alarmingly and the Bechuanaland Protectorate Government formed the Elephant Control Unit to cull the herd.

Major Pat Bromfield was in command and Simon Holmes a' Court was his assistant, and over a period of ten years, about 1 800 elephants were shot between the Shashe and Motloutse Rivers. The two men not only kept the elephant under control, but were instrumental in the formation of the

41. Ilona Somerset. Born on: 19/05/1951. Died on: 15/02/1999, 47 years old. Lived in: Selebi Phikwe, Central Botswana.

National Parks in Botswana. The Elephant Control Unit became the Game Department, the forerunner of the Department of Wildlife and National Parks. The two Game Department men rendered invaluable service to the Rhodesian Schools Exploration Society expeditions to Fort Tuli and Fort Matlaputla. Major Bromfield "discovered" the ruins of Fort Matlaputla in 1959, and on this expedition Simon Holmes a' Court was bitten by a puff -adder (*Bitis arietans*). The bite was very painful and the men were given an insight into the clinical symptoms of snake-bite. The incident undoubtedly dampened their youthful enthusiasm for herpetology.

Major Bromfield retired from the Game Department to live in Perth, Australia. Simon Holmes a' Court turned his talents and skills to the art of wildlife sculpture and his work received high critical acclaim. He disappeared without trace whilst on holiday in the Garden Route. The authorities found his car at the Storms River Bridge with the engine number obliterated. Years later human skeletal remains were found in the forest and it is assumed that these are the remains of Simon Holmes a' Court.

Today more than 700 elephant live in the Northern Reserve and a small herd wanders from the reserve along the Motloutse and Sedibe Rivers. The land in South Africa proclaimed by Jan Smuts was de-gazetted when his Nationalist opponents in the Northern Transvaal, led by JG Strijdom, promised farmers the land if they voted the Nat ticket in 1948. Smuts lost his premiership and his game reserve. Talks between Zimbabwe, South Africa and Botswana began in 1995 to discuss the proclamation of a large game area. Incorporation of the Tuli Enclave in Botswana, the Tuli Trust in Zimbabwe, Venetia Diamond Reserve and the farms on the South African side of the Limpopo into an international game reserve is on the agenda.

When George Adamson was murdered in Kenya, his pupil in lion rehabilitation, Gareth Patterson, brought the last of the Adamson lions to the Tuli Block. The move is not without controversy. One of the lions was allegedly lured onto the South African side and shot by a farmer, who claimed it was killing his stock. A second lion is allegedly responsible for attacking and killing a tracker at Mashatu, although Patterson vehemently denies this charge. He claims that the tracker Isaac Mangagola was murdered because he knew something about poaching in the area.

The lion's share of the land is owned by Mashatu, which is flanked by Tuli Lodge and private consortiums like Jwala and Charter. The reserve is not fenced and the game moves freely on the 160 000 acre enclave between the Shashe and Motloutse Rivers. It does not boast all of the Big Five. Buffalo were wiped out by foot-and-mouth disease many years ago, and rhino were exterminated by hunters and trekkers before the turn of the 20th century. However, the reserve has wonderful prides of lion, groups of cheetah and abundant leopard, and it is home to the largest single population of elephant on private land in the world. General game abounds and the area harbours the most magnificent variety of birds, with over 400 species recorded.

Skeletal remains of the thin greyhound-like "traditional dogs" of Botswana have been found at human settlements dating to the Leopard's Koppie period. Although not registered as a breed by the Kennel Union, traditional dogs serve their masters as herders, hunting hounds, watch-dogs and pets. Young puppies are suckled by nanny goats and grow up believing they are goats, but they immediately assume authority over the flock. The dogs sleep in the goat kraal at night, and when they bestir themselves they lead the goats to the bush. Whilst the goats graze, the dogs lounge in the shade of trees. As sunset approaches, the dogs return to the village, followed faithfully by the goats and, according to the farmers, dogs are more reliable than herd boys. As the village borders a game area, attacks by caracul, leopard, jackal and hyena are not uncommon, but goat-dogs will counter-attack by barking and jumping backwards and forwards, creating a shower of pebbles. The predators usually withdraw in total surprise at the sudden ferocity of the "goats", and when a goat is in serious trouble the goat-dogs bay in a certain manner to alert the villagers. The goat-dogs remain with a stricken goat until the villagers, guided by the barks of the dogs, arrive to drive off the attackers.

The village of Lentswe le Moriti has an interesting background. Kgosi Molefi Kgafela of the Bakgatla in Mochudi decided to end the conflict between the Dutch Reformed Church, the Zion Christian Church and himself by banishing the Zion Christian Church from Mochudi. The adherents to the ZCC and their families lived at the edge of the railway line and after six months they were removed to Gaborone Siding, near the present station, whilst the authorities decided what to do with them.

They hired a Zeerust lawyer named Coulson to seek land for them. Coulson tried to buy land in the Gaberone's Block but was frustrated by the protest of white farmers. After attempts to find land in the Tati District and the Molopo Farms, he obtained the farm Loensa le Moridi in the Tuli Block, and after five years of wandering and wondering the Zionists reached their Canaan in 1952. The village has some examples of traditional housing and the kgotla is, at time of writing, a traditional palisade.

THE MOKOLWANE WINE ROUTE

This is the only wine route in Botswana, but the estates of the Cape are safe from serious competition. There is not much to see other than the tapping of the wine, and tasting is not guaranteed. However, a visit to the rock paintings at Motlhabaneng would not be complete without a visit to the Tap Winery. The sap in the Fan Palm (*Hyphaene petersiana*) increases in volume just before flowering time. The wine-maker burns the area surrounding the tree to rid it of extra growth, and the heat increases the sap. After burning, the remaining leaves are cut away until only the stem is left. About 10 cm of stem protrudes from the ground and an incision is made near the top. A palm leaf is inserted and the sap runs down the blade for collection in bottles. To protect the wine against insects and animals, the wine-maker weaves a basket and covers the bottle. Palm wine is delicious in its fresh state and tastes like ginger beer. It is mildly intoxicating in its fresh state, but if left to ferment for 24 to 36 hours it becomes effervescent and rather strong. However, when the Babirwa learned the art of distillation the character of Mokolwane Wine altered completely.

The cemetery at Fort Tuli tells many a tragic tale. Fever and dysentery were the main causes of death, but some met their Maker by accident, like Trooper Theodore Cumberlege Fenton. The nearest distillery of conventional gin and brandy was at Marico, 900 kilometres distant, and without the palm there would have been many sober and thirsty days in camp. Known as Tuli Firewater or Bobirwa London Dry Gin, the distilled spirit was raw and downright dangerous. Soldiers relieved the tedium of waiting for orders or something to happen through the spirit-building liquor bottle, the British South Africa Company's Police and Bechuanaland Border Police were no exception.

Fenton and friends enjoyed a rip-roaring hoolie one night and the troopers passed out in their small pup tents. Awaking some hours later in discomfort from a full bladder, Fenton crawled out of his tent to relieve the pressure. He tripped over his dog and, in temper, gave the cur a swift kick in the flanks. He erred, for it was not Fido at the receiving end of the wrathful trooper's foot but a fully grown lion. It took understandable umbrage at this unexpected and unwarranted attack and retaliated with leonine ferocity. The Late Trooper Fenton was buried with full military honours in Tuli cemetery. Distillation of Bobirwa London Dry Gin is highly illegal, but it is still practised. A Mobirwa friend "acquired" some for me to taste and I can truthfully assert that when NASA gets to utilise it, fuel costs on the Space Shuttle will be considerably reduced.

Unfortunately, tapping trees for wine reduces their life span and some trees die after only two seasons of production. The palm fruit has a hard ivory-coloured pip that locals use for buttons or carve into ornaments. Botswana baskets are much sought after, but most weaving takes place in the Okavango Swamps. The quality of basket weaving improved with the immigration of the Hambukushu from Angola to the Okavango, and Babirwa women have attended workshops to learn the art. Once they are fully trained, their art will be on sale in Bobonong, the Tuli Block, Selebi-Phikwe and at roadside stalls on the Martin's Drift Road.

The Motlhabaneng Hills are sandstone ridges stretching for forty kilometres and the eroded formations are exceptionally attractive. Hidden in an amphitheatre of sandstone walls is the art gallery of Motlhabaneng. The elephant paintings are low on the rock face and they are very clear. The second part of the gallery is an overhang concealed by a large rock. This mural has giraffe, wildebeest, antbear, impala and zebra. Sadly, vandals have damaged a couple of paintings by scratching over them. Another painting shows giraffe, elephant, impala and buffalo.

A magnificent iron bridge spans the Motloutse at Motlhabaneng. The bridge is wide enough for only one vehicle and there is a footbridge attached. A lattice work of metal forms the bridge sides and the surface is made of slabs of cast metal similar to the Bailey Bridges used during World War II. The Bakwena Company of the Bechuanaland Protectorate forces serving in the Italian Campaign erected the longest Bailey Bridge used during the war, a half-mile structure over the Sangro River.

Human settlement in the Northern Reserve dates to the Leopard's Koppie Culture. The main city at Mapungubwe is on the South African side of the border. This immense site has been under archaeological research by the University of Pretoria since the 1930s[42].

Close to the ruin is a large baobab tree that has the initials CJR, or Cecil John Rhodes, and it can be assumed that this was carved in the summer of 1893. Just above the CJR is a carving ADC which may be Antonio de la Cruz, Rhodes valet and personal servant who travelled everywhere with his boss. There is a faint carving of a Bechuanaland Border Police trooper and crossed swords in the bark.

THE TULI CIRCLE

Both the Ngwato and the Ndebele claimed the area between the Shashe and Motloutse Rivers, and to avoid conflict neither nation inhabited nor grazed cattle in the area. Selous and his Mongwato assistant Makamana selected a site on the south bank of the Shashe within the Disputed Territory for the site of Fort Tuli. In 1892 Lungsickness or contagious bovine pleuro-pneumonia broke out in Gammangwato, and King Khama III granted the ten mile radius to the Chartered Company as a disease control barrier. Popular legend that Rhodes fired cannon shots and laid the Circle where the balls landed is completely unfounded. A cannon with a ten-mile range and cannon balls that do not shatter on impact had not yet been invented in 1892.

The Tuli Circle was ceded in 1899 to the British South Africa Company because Fort Tuli, one of the Company's main police posts, lay within the

42. *Mapungubwe Ancient Bantu Civilization on the Limpopo Reports on Excavations at Mapungubwe (Northern Transvaal) from February 1933 to June 1935,* Fouche, Leo (edited on behalf of the Archaelogical Committee of the University or Pretoria), Published by Cambridge University Press, Cambridge UK, 1937.

Circle. Fort Tuli was a British South Africa Police post for many years and the only place that the Game Department men on elephant cull could get a cold beer. The British South Africa Company's Police had a Heliograph Signal Station at Baobab Spruit near Lone Tree Hill and this baobab is a living monument of historical carvings.

LIMPOPO AND SHASHE RIVER CONFLUENCE

In the North-east corner of the Northern reserve is the confluence of the Limpopo and Shashe Rivers. During the 1960s, a British South Africa Police Inspector named Cherry decided he had had enough of Police work at his Fort Tuli base. He erected a flag-pole on the island, declared UDI and proclaimed himself President-for-Life. Visitors were not welcome and all trespassers were shot on sight. Happily the Inspector's aim was faulty and no-one was hurt. Cherry was removed after about three months of Independence and his flag was lowered for the last time. The flag-pole still stands, but the whereabouts of the British South Africa Policeman is unknown. The vegetation around the confluence is magnificent. In addition to Mashatu there are huge baobabs and plenty of fan palms.

PONT DRIFT

Guarding the drifts on the Limpopo against possible Boer invasion was the main task of the British South Africa Company's Police. Main Drift was near Beit Bridge and Middle Drift roughly half way between Pont Drift and Main Drift. Pont Drift was the most convenient entry point for Mashonaland-bound traffic from the Transvaal. CH Zeederberg, fondly known as Doel, was awarded a Mail Contract by the Transvaal government, with the proviso that his coach service would use the road from Pretoria to the drift via Nylstroom. The Mail Contractor placed a ferry at the

Limpopo to keep his mail coaches moving when the river was flooded. The Transvaal Government appointed a customs officer at the drift. On the Botswana side, patrols from Fort Tuli were regularly changed to guard the entrance to Mashonaland.

The origin of the name Pont Drift is obvious, but if legend is to be believed, President Kruger gave orders that the post station and store on the Transvaal side would be called Hendrikzdal, after the incumbent customs officer. Drink is usually the chief source of a quarrel and whilst E Troop of the British South Africa Company's Police was waiting for the orders to march to Fort Matlaputla, hours were spent in the company of a bottle. At Isaac's Store in Mafikeng one night, a new trooper known only as Hendrik, bragged about how many Rooinekke he had killed at the Battle of Majuba and made mockery of the easy target presented by a Rooinek soldier. Not unnaturally, a brawl broke out between Home-Born and staunch Colonials, and Hendrik was discharged and promptly forgotten. British South Africa Company's Police officers and men were astonished to learn six months later that the customs official at Hendrikzdal was none other than the despised Trooper Hendrik.

The Adendorf Trek caused much concern on the border in 1891, when the trekkers gathered in Pietersburg. The trek threat started soon after the Assent to the Charter of the British South Africa Company when Kruger decided to play the safety in numbers game. With *trekgees* and the desire to find the Promised Land still running high in Boer emotions, trekkers packed their wagons and gathered at Pietersburg in large numbers. There they hung around waiting for orders to inspan and trek. Doel Zeederberg's mail coach passed through the town in 1891 en route to Fort Tuli and the coach contractor was unconvinced that the trek would actually move. He told Major Leonard, the garrison commander at Fort Tuli, that there was no chance of a move as the trekkers were disagreed about key issues such as place of settlement. A two-wagon party of Englishmen were also convinced that the trek would not advance.

Sir Henry Loch thought otherwise and proved why he was such a good Governor. He ordered all drifts over the Limpopo to be manned and Major Sir John Willoughby arrived at Tuli to take command. At once he ordered heavy firepower at each drift and tried to make the fort itself impregnable. None of the forts in Botswana and Zimbabwe were any use against firepower, as they were designed to keep the assegai-armed Ndebele out and not Boer sharpshooters, but apparently Willoughby did not recognise the fact.

As the Commander at Fort Tuli Captain Arthur Leonard put it, there was no way of knowing in this country what an hour may bring, and soon Willougby was on his way back to Manicaland and Major Hamilton Goold-Adams arrived from Macloutsie with an appointment to take over command. It was the better appointment. Diplomacy and tact were likely to win over Boer confidence rather than fire power and bluster. Besides, the odds were very much against the combined forces of the Bechuanaland Border Police and British South Africa Company's Police. Goold-Adams was better suited to the task of diplomacy than Willoughby, who, it was rumoured, had talked carelessly in Pretoria about the proposed trek.

Jameson, the Doctor-turned-Diplomat, arrived at Fort Tuli on the Zeederberg Coach on 3 June 1891. Lieutenant Crichton-Browne turned up with twenty-eight Bechuanaland Border Police troopers and Lieutenant Flowers brought a further sixty-four troopers and five wagons to reinforce the drifts.

A week after Jameson arrived at Fort Tuli, a telegram was received announcing the arrival of Colonel Sir Frederick Carrington, the officer commanding all forces in Mashonaland and the Protectorate for an inspection tour. Apparently he did not expect a fight with Boers or he would have been on the spot to take command much earlier. When Leonard mentioned the commanding officer's intention, Jameson's rejoinder was caustic. "Yes," he remarked, "a good excuse to meet Lord Randolph Churchill, and have a shoot and a free drink."

The attempted trek was all over without a shout or a shot on 28 June 1891. About two hundred trekkers arrived at Main Drift on the 24th. At the time the only officer at the drift was Surgeon-Lieutenant Goody. After all the preparation and fuss to keep the Boers out, when the crunch came it was left to a doctor. Goody sent men to call Goold-Adams with all speed and arrested Ignatius Ferreira, who had already crossed the drift.

Jameson turned up shortly afterwards and a meeting was held between him and the trek leaders, who were told that entry into Mashonaland would bind them to Chartered Company rule. Jameson called their bluff and most of them went home. A sprinkling, including Ferreira, agreed to abide by Company Law and the Boers were given leave to proceed. Subsequent treks were quite orderly and no further attempt were made to invade

Lord Randolph Churchill, the first private citizen to visit Mashonaland, arrived at Rhodes' Drift in his mule-drawn Spider on 12 July 1891. Captain Lawrie of the Bechuanaland Border Police escorted the peer on the Zeederberg Road to Fort Tuli, where he was hospitably entertained by Colonel Sir Frederick Carrington, Major Leonard, Major Goold-Adams and troopers of the British South Africa Company's Police and Bechuanaland Border Police.

Lord Randolph was born at his ancestral home, Blenheim Palace, with a gem-encrusted gold spoon in his mouth. An error of birth denied him the title of Marquess of Blandford and heir to the Duchy of Marlbourgh, but he was no loafer or fool. He was only twenty-six years old when he was elected to Parliament and his rare gift of satirical oratory took him up speedily through the corridors and up the stairs of power. At thirty-six he was Secretary of State for India; the following year he became Chancellor of the Exchequer. His meteoric rise in English politics rewarded him with many enemies and his miscalculation of public opinion did not, as he expected, bring down the Government, but it forced him to resign.

Lord Randolph married a New York socialite Jenny Jerome in 1874 and their first child, Winston, who would succeed in politics where his father failed, was born in the same year. By 1891 Lord Randolph was allegedly in the tertiary stages of syphilis, a condition which may have contributed to his political misjudgement. He was a shareholder in the British South Africa Company and, disenchanted with politics and Society, he decided to visit Mashonaland and view the Company prospects.

Southern Africa is yet to host another tourist equal to Lord Randolph. He complained about the poor cuisine in Klerksdorp; he criticised the Raadzaal in Pretoria; and his closing remarks on the Boers would be neither forgiven nor forgotten. Lord Randolph described the Boer as "a perfectly uneducated personification of useless idleness, with an implicit belief of every word written in the Bible. Furthermore, he is unambitious and prefers to have his children grow up as uneducated, uncultivated and ignorant as himself." There were, he conceded, a few bright exceptions, but he wrote further, "I rejoiced after all I had seen in the Transvaal, that the country and the people of Matabeleland and Mashonaland had been rescued in the nick of time, owing to the genius of Mr. Rhodes and the tardy vigour of the British Government from the withering and mortal grasp of the Boer." Small wonder then, that when Winston was captured at Chievelly during the Boer War, the Boers were overwhelmed with joy and they made his life in captivity very unpleasant. When Prime Minister Jan Smuts called for volunteers in response to Sir Winston Churchill's speeches in World War II, Lord Randolph's remarks were resurrected and the call to arms was largely ignored by Afrikaners.

Lord Randolph travelled to Tuli through the Transvaal, whilst his wagons went on the Pioneer Road and rendezvoused at Fort Tuli. The Transport Contractor owned Southern Africa's most beloved dog, Jock, and in later years he would claim to be the first South African - Sir Percy Fitzpatrick. Churchill's articles in the *Daily Graphic*, for which he was paid 2000 Guineas, raised the ire of the British South Africa Company. He saw no future in European settlement, nor did he view the gold prospects with enthusiasm, but despite the criticism he did not refuse Rhodes's hospitality at Groote Schuur in Cape Town. When censured by a friend, Lord Randolph replied, "My dear fellow, it's the only place in this God-forsaken country where I can get Perrier Jouet '74."

THE BATTLE OF BRYCE'S STORE

The strategic importance of the railway was never lost on the Boers. Just before the outbreak of the Boer War, Danie Theron, the famous Boer Scout, loaded his bicycle on the train at Mafikeng and left for Bulawayo to assess the military strength in the town. It was his intention to cycle back via Tuli and Macloutsie as a prospective settler, but when war broke out he decided to take the safer route via Main Drift. Near Pietersburg he fell off his bicycle and split his trousers; the bike was irreparable, but he fixed his trousers by making pins from acacia thorn and had an uncomfortable and perilous walk to Pretoria.

Mafikeng was placed under siege and Colonel Herbert Plumer mustered a force of colonial irregulars to defend the Protectorate and the fledgling

Rhodesia from a base at Fort Tuli. The first fighting took place in October 1899 at Pont Drift, where a small commando crossed the river and took up position on a koppie overlooking the main road to Tuli. A foot patrol was ambushed, killing Sergeant-Major Yonge. The Boers, commanded by Veld-Kornet Briel, marched to Rhodes' Drift and were attacked from the rear by Captain Leslie Blackburn of the Scottish Regiment and eight troopers. In the skirmish Blackburn was wounded and three or four troopers taken prisoner. Blackburn died later of his wounds and was buried with honours in the Fort Tuli Cemetery

On 28th October 1899, Lieutenant-Colonel the Hon H White, now restored to rank after his part in the Jameson Raid, carried out a foot reconnaissance with Captain Glynn and forty men. By day-break they were two hundred yards from the koppie at Rhodes' Drift and were attacked by a mounted commando, but drove them off with return fire. From the koppie the patrol was again attacked, and in the skirmish Lieutenant Hutchinson and three troopers were wounded. The Boers are said to have lost a Veld-Kornet and some men. A force under Major Pilson, who had survived the first attack, was placed on a low ridge overlooking Rhodes' Drift. From the summit there is a clear view of the drift marshland and the Zeederberg Road. Major W. Bird was posted to Solomon's Wall, from whence he commanded a view over the Limpopo River Valley, and his troops camped under the wall itself. Captain K. McLaren was posted to Macloutsie, although the abandoned fort was not likely to be attacked; it was of strategic importance because the Pioneer Road was the only access to the south. Pilson's command was short as Plumer replaced him with Colonel Jack Spreckley, a former Paymaster Sergeant in the Pioneer Corps. Before withdrawing, Pilson burned all fodder and left nothing that could sustain the enemy.

Van Rensburg, the Boer General in command of the Northern Transvaal, waited for reinforcements. The intention was to destroy all garrisons from Baines' Drift to Fort Tuli and weaken the British hold over Rhodesia. Sarel Eloff of the Zoutpansberg Commando and SP Grobler, a Police commander, reinforced the Boers who were encamped at Hendrikzdal.

About nine kilometres from Rhodes' Drift was Bryce's Store, a supply point for troopers at Solomon's Wall and Rhodes' Drift. The proprietor was known to his best customers, the Babirwa, as Mahlongwenya because he shot many crocodiles in the Limpopo River. The store was built of dagha bricks and roofed with corrugated iron, and it had a shady veranda in the front, where many a cold beer was consumed by bored troopers.

Spreckley, now in command of the ridge at Rhodes' Drift, had no supplies, so a convoy of six mule-drawn wagons was despatched from Fort Tuli under escort of Lieutenants Hare and Haserick, six Rhodesia Regiment troopers and six from the British South Africa Police. The escort was accompanied by the Anglican Chaplain, the Rev. J. Leary, who saw this as an opportunity to visit his flock at Rhodes' Drift.

On Thursday, 2 November 1899, van Rensburg made his move, crossing the river at Rhodes' Drift with three hundred mounted men and three cannon. Van Rensburg, Grobler and Veld-Kornet Kelly engaged Spreckley on the ridge, shelling the British encampment from a distance of 500 metres with a seven-pounder and a Hotchkiss. The only casualties occurred when the horse kraal took a direct hit.

Whilst Spreckley was kept busy, Eloff and Veld-Kornets Briel and Alberts sneaked around and mounted a ridge overlooking Bryce's Store and the Pitsane River. A 1½ metre wide and two metre high breastwork was constructed of rocks to protect the seven-pounder. A shallow trench for riflemen was dug and the Hotchkiss was probably located at one corner of the trench.

At about midday the convoy arrived at Bryce's Store and went inside for brunch. They had scarcely swallowed the first mouthful when the Boer infantry opened fire from about one thousand yards. The fire was returned and the Boers got within two hundred yards of the store. Then all hell broke loose. The artillery opened accurate fire and blew the roof off the building and the occupants were forced to surrender. Haserick and Leary were wounded and taken prisoner. Leary's wounds were treated by Mrs. Sue Nicholson, who used a wagon as a field hospital at Hendrikzdal.

Outnumbered and outgunned, Spreckley's men withdrew in single file, leaving on the ridge all their kit and saddlery, taking a north-easterly course to avoid the road, which was in Boer control. After a sixteen-hour march without rations or water they arrived at the Shashe, where they met Pilson, who handed over his horses to the footsore troopers.

There was no further action during the Boer War in the Northern Tuli Block. The remains of the Boer stone breastwork and trench can still be seen on the ridge overlooking Bryce's Store. The kop was also an Iron Age Smelting site. Potsherds are scattered about in great numbers and I noticed globs of smelted metal on the summit. An almost-whole pot is embedded in the ground close to the cannon breastwork. Not a lot remains of Bryce's Store and it is believed that Mr. Bryce cleared off shortly after the attack and set up a store near Lake Malawi. The foundations of the store, rondavel and veranda can still be seen and a few broken bits of tin, crockery and glass are evidence of late-19th century human activity. Veld-Kornet Tom Kelly was captured by the Australian Bushveldt Carbineers near Bandolierkop towards the end of the war. His arrest was the last official duty of his captors - Lieutenants "Breaker" Morant and Peter Handcock.

The British South Africa Company's Police stronghold at Rhodes Drift is a great sundowner outspan on a Mashatu game drive. The small ridge commands a view of the flat open vlei and the riverine trees of the Limpopo. The sunset is glorious from this wild place and guests are often rewarded with sundown game sightings. I saw spent Mauser bullets, Lee Enfield cartridge cases and the usual bits of tin and glass. Someone enjoyed Holland's Gin and Roses Lime Juice at Rhodes' Drift in the 1890s. I saw fragments of a square-faced gin bottle and detected the trade mark of Roses Lime Juice on a piece of glass.

The Zeederberg Road via Pont Drift was considerably shorter than other routes to Mashonaland, but most settlers opted for the Pioneer Road and Missionaries Road to avoid trekking through Boer territory. Like the other wagon trails, it fell into disuse at the turn of the century. The modern adventurer should ask his ranger to arrange a game drive on this historical trail.

LORD LUCAN LEGEND

In November 1974, Sandra Rivett was found murdered in the basement of a London house. She had been bludgeoned to death. An all-out man-hunt for Richard John Bingham, the 7th Earl of Lucan, was ordered and the hunt has persisted ever since. Lord Lucan has been tried, found guilty and sentenced in books, newspapers, television and even at an inquest. It has been alleged that the peer committed suicide after the murder, but no bodily remains have ever been found. Lately, the missing Lord Lucan has been "seen" in Gaborone, Francistown and the Tuli Block. The remoteness and exclusivity of the Tuli Block allegedly makes the ideal refuge for a fugitive, and a Scotland Yard Inspector came out of retirement to follow up leads that Lucan was hiding in the Tuli Block. It may be a vast and remote area, but like any place with a small population, gossip spreads faster than a bush fire and secrets are poorly kept in the Tuli Block.

Lord Lucan is still wanted for questioning, but as the press has already convicted him, he stands no chance in a court of law and he is better off in exile, wherever that may be. With respect to the victim, one cannot be sure that such attention would be given if Joe Bloggs had done in a tart and hidden in the Tuli Block. Let Lord Lucan lie and lose the legend.

* * *

Cable car basket at Pont Drift border post

Fan Palms

Troops garrisoned at Fort Tuli, 1890 (Photo Ellerton Fry)

Bibliography

Brandon-Kirby, Robert, *Fly-Fishing in Southern Africa*, Struik Winchester, Cape Town, 1993.

Dachs, AJ, *Missionary Imperialism, the case of Bechuanaland*, Journal of African History, Vol 13, 1972.

Durbach, Renee, *Kipling's South Africa*, Chameleon Press, Hong Kong, 1988.

FitzPatrick, P, *South African Memories*, Cassel, London, 1932.

Hilton-Barber, David, *The Baronet and the Matabele King, The Intriguing Story of the Tati Concession*, 30 Degrees South, Durban, 2015.

Keane, AH, *The Boer States: Land and People*, Methuen, London, 1900.

Kipling, Rudyard, *Something of Myself: For my Friends Known and Unknown,* Macmillan, Loondon, 1937.

Levy, Andrew, *The Magic Valley, Freshwater Fish and Fishing in Africa*, Nelson, 1963.

Metrowich, FC, *Scotty Smith*, Books of Africa, Cape Town, 1983.

Paulin, Christopher, *White Men's Dreams, Black Men's Blood: African Labour and British Expansionism in Southern Africa, 1877-1895*, Africa World Press, Trenton USA, 2001.

Rae, C, *Notes from my Diary on the Boer campaign of 1894 against the chief Malaboch of Blaauwberg, district Zoutpansberg, South African Republic,* Juta, Johannesburg, 1898.

Ramsay, J, *The Establishment and Consolidation of the Bechuanaland Protectorate, 1877- 1910*

Somerset, Ilona, *The Seven Lost Trails And Outdoor Adventures In Eastern Botswana*, unpublished.

Theal, George McCall, *History of South Africa 1873-1884*, C. Struik, 1964.

Wallace, G, *Religion and Afrikaner Nationalism*. Mills Hist. 322 14a.

Webb, C, *Uitlander Movement in the South African Republic before the Jameson Raid*, presented for his BA Honours degree at the University of the Witwatersrand, 1952.

www.ingramcontent.com/pod-product-compliance
Lightning Source LLC
LaVergne TN
LVHW090951080826
845145LV00003B/964

* 9 7 8 0 6 2 0 7 8 4 6 8 9 *